THE OFFICIAL MTO
TRUCK HANDBOOK

This handbook is only a guide. For official purposes, please refer to the *Ontario Highway Traffic Act* and regulations, the *Dangerous Goods Act* and *Federal Motor Vehicle Transport Act*.

For more information about driver licensing, visit www.mto.gov.on.ca. See the *Official MTO Driver's Handbook* for information on Ontario rules of the road.

To request a copy of this book in an alternate format, contact Publications Ontario at 1-800-668-9938 or (416) 326-5300, or visit www.publications.serviceontario.ca

Disponible en français
Demandez le « Guide offici

DRIVING IS A PRIVIL

D1089676

1

INTRODUCTION

The Ministry of Transportation (MTO) is committed to making Ontario's roads safer for everyone. Ontario is a leader in truck safety standards and enforcement, with some of the toughest safety laws in North America. The province has approximately 58,000 commercial carriers actively operating on Ontario's roadways.

Ontario has announced mandatory entry-level training for new Commercial Class A truck drivers. Individuals seeking a Class A licence in Ontario need to successfully complete mandatory entry-level training before attempting the Class A road test, effective July 1, 2017. Individuals who already have a Class A licence will not be required to take training. Applicants for a Class A or D licence will also be taking a newly updated road and knowledge tests.

The initial knowledge test has been rewritten to accommodate these changes. The information you will need to know for the new knowledge and road test has been included in this handbook.

Some improvements you may notice include a new chapter called The Road Test, plus expanded information on backing, roundabout and load security.

The mandatory entry-level course will take approximately four to six weeks to complete, with course content by a ministry-approved provider.

This handbook is designed to help people applying for a Class A or D driver's licence. It contains the information you need to meet the standards for those licences, and sets out the skills you will be expected to perform during a driving test. It also outlines the many safety initiatives the ministry has introduced, as well as detailing the best practices for safe and responsible operation of a commercial vehicle.

The information in this book is only a guide to help a new driver understand the basic rules, legislation and regulation in the province. For further details, consult the *Highway Traffic Act* and its regulations.

Drive safely

CONTENTS

CONTENTS

CHAPTER 1
GETTING YOUR LICENCE

I. LEGISLATION

These Acts and regulations govern truck driving in Ontario.

1. *The Highway Traffic Act (HTA)* and the following regulations govern the driver, the vehicle and equipment, weight and numbers of passengers that a driver can carry: Commercial Motor Vehicle Inspections Reg. 199/07; Commercial Motor Vehicle Operators' Information Reg. 424/97; Covering of Loads R.R.O.1990. Reg.577; Critical Defects of Commercial Motor Vehicles O.Reg.512/97; Equipment R.R.O.1990. Reg.587; Hours of Service O.Reg.555/06; Safety Inspections R.R.O.1990.Reg.611; Security of Loads O.Reg.363/04; Definitions of Commercial Motor Vehicle and Tow Truck Reg. 419/15.

2. *Dangerous Goods Transportation Act* regulates the transportation of dangerous goods, including required documentation, handling, safety markings (labels and placards) and the certification of drivers.

Transporting dangerous goods

There are nine classes of dangerous goods ranging from corrosives and flammable liquids to environmentally hazardous materials. Drivers transporting dangerous goods must receive training from their current employer. The employer determines the level of training required. Once trainingis successfully completed, the employer issues the driver a certificate that must be carried when transporting dangerous goods.

For further information on dangerous goods training, visit the Transport Canada website: www.tc.gc.ca.

DRIVER'S LICENCE CLASSIFICATION CHART

Class of License		Types of vehicles allowed	May also drive vehicles in class
A		Any tractor-trailer combination	D and G
B		Any school-purposes bus	C, D, E, F and G
C		Any regular bus	D, F and G
D		A motor vehicle exceeding 11,000 kilograms gross weight or registered gross weight or any truck or combination provided the towed vehicle is not over 4,600 kilograms	G
E		School-purposes bus – maximum of 24-passenger capacity	F and G
F		Regular bus – maximum of 24-passenger capacity – and ambulances	G

Diagram 1-1a

Class of License

G 		Allowed to drive any car, van or small truck or combination of vehicle and towed vehicle up to 11,000 kilograms provided the towed vehicle is not over 4,600 kilograms. A pickup truck towing a house trailer exceeds 4,600 kilograms but the total combined weight of the truck and trailer does not exceed 11,000 kilograms is deemed a Class G.
G1		Level One of graduated licensing. Holders may drive Class G vehicles with an accompanying fully licensed driver with at least four years' driving experience. Subject to certain conditions.
G2		Level Two of graduated licensing. Holders may drive Class G vehicles without accompanying driver but are subject to certain conditions.
M		Allowed to drive any motorcycles, including motor tricycles, limited-speed motorcycles (motor scooters) and motor-assisted bicycles (mopeds). Holders may also drive a Class G vehicle under the conditions that apply to a Class G1 licence holder.
M1		Level One of graduated licensing for motorcycles, including motor tricycles, limited-speed motorcycles (motor scooters) and motor-assisted bicycles (mopeds). Holders may drive a motorcycle under certain conditions.
M2		Level Two of graduated licensing for motorcycles, including motor tricycles, limited-speed motorcycles (motor scooters) and motor-assisted bicycles (mopeds). Holders may drive a motorcycle but only with a zero blood-alcohol level. Holders may also drive a Class G vehicle under the conditions that apply to a Class G1 licence holder.
M with L condition 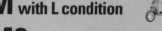		Holders may operate a limited-speed motorcycle or moped only.
M2 with L condition		Holders may operate a limited-speed motorcycle or moped only.
M with M condition 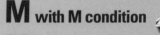		Holders may operate a motor tricycle only.
M2 with M condition 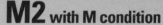		Holders may operate a motor tricycle only.

Diagram 1-1b

Note: A "Z" air brake endorsement is required on a driver's licence to operate any air brake equipped motor vehicle.

II. DEFINITIONS

Commercial motor vehicle: unless otherwise defined by regulation, means a motor vehicle having attached to it a truck or delivery body and includes an ambulance, a hearse, a casket wagon, a fire apparatus, a bus and a tractor used for hauling purposes on a highway.

Gross weight: the combined weight of vehicle and load.

Registered gross weight: the weight for which a permit has been issued under the *HTA*; the fee for the permit is based upon the weight of the vehicle or combination of vehicles and load.

Manufacturers' gross vehicle weight rating (MGVWR): the gross weight as specified by the manufacturer; often attached as a decal or plate on the cab of a vehicle.

Motor vehicle: an automobile, motorcycle, motor-assisted bicycle and any other vehicle propelled or driven other than by muscular power. Not included are the cars of electric or steam railways or other motor vehicles running only upon rails; motorized snow vehicles; traction engines; farm tractors; power-assisted bikes; or road-building machines.

Semi-trailer: a trailer designed to be operated with the forward part of its body or chassis resting upon the body or chassis of a towing vehicle.

Trailer: a vehicle drawn, propelled or moved by a motor vehicle. The definition does not include farm implements, mobile homes, motor vehicles, side cars attached to motorcycles, or any device not designed to transport persons or property. A trailer is considered a separate vehicle and not part of the motor vehicle by which it is drawn.

Vehicle: a motor vehicle, trailer, traction engine, farm tractor, roadbuilding machine or any vehicle drawn, propelled or driven by any kind of power, including muscular power. The definition does not include motorized snow vehicles or the cars of electric or steam railways running only upon rails.

Self-propelled implement of husbandry: a self-propelled vehicle used specifically in farming, such as a farm tractor.

III. A AND D LICENCE CLASSES AND REQUIREMENTS

The Driver's Licence Classification Chart on pages 8 to 9 shows you what class of licence you need to drive different types of vehicles. A licensed driver wishing to learn to operate a truck or tractor-trailer must hold a class G or higher driver's licence and be accompanied by a driver who holds a valid class D or class A licence, respectively. Your driving competence will be assessed in a road test held at a DriveTest Centre; or an employer or community college authorized by the Ministry of Transportation (known as a Recognized Authority) may assess you on the road test and issue a certificate of driving competence for classes A, B, C, D, E, F and M. You may then obtain the appropriate driver's licence from the ministry.

The class A driver's licence allows you to drive a motor vehicle and towed vehicles where the towed vehicles exceed a total gross weight of 4,600 kilograms (10,000 lb); and vehicles included in classes D and G. A class A licence does not permit you to drive a bus carrying passengers, a motorcycle or a moped.

Class A vehicles are considered to have either full configuration or restricted configuration as defined below.

Full Class A Vehicle Configuration
- Any combination of truck/tractor and trailer with a Manufacturer's Gross Vehicle Weight Rating (MGVWR) of at least 4600 kg; and
- A full air brake system on both the truck/ tractor and trailer.

Restricted Class A Configuration
- Any combination of truck/tractor and trailer with a Manufacturer's Gross Vehicle Weight Rating (MGVWR) of at least 4600 kg; and
- Trailer is not equipped with air brakes.

A driver completing a Class "A" road test on a vehicle that does not meet the requirement for a full Class "A" vehicle will be issued an AR (A Restricted) licence and will not be able to operate a full Class "A" vehicle.

The class D driver's licence allows you to drive a motor vehicle exceeding 11,000 kilograms (24,000 lb) gross weight or registered gross weight, or any combination of motor vehicle exceeding a total gross weight or registered gross weight of 11,000 kilograms (24,000 lb) and towed vehicle not exceeding a total gross weight of 4,600 kilograms (10,000 lb). It also allows you to operate vehicles in class G. A class D licence does not permit you to drive a bus carrying passengers, a motorcycle or a moped.

Minimum requirements for Class A or D driver's licence application:

An applicant for a class A or D driver's licence must:
- Be at least 18 years of age
- Hold a valid Ontario class G or higher licence or equivalent

- Pass a test of operating knowledge of large trucks and tractor trailers
- Meet vision standards
- Provide a satisfactory medical certificate on application and periodically thereafter
- Demonstrate driving competence during a road test while driving the following types of vehicles:
  - For class D – A motor vehicle exceeding 11,000 kilograms gross weight or registered gross weight or any truck or combination provided the towed vehicle is not over 4,600 kilograms
  - For class A – a motor vehicle and towed vehicle where the towed vehicle exceeds a total gross weight of 4,600 kilograms (10,000 lb)

Medical certificate

When applying for a class A or D licence, you must provide a completed satisfactory ministry medical certificate. Blank medical forms can be obtained from any DriveTest Centre in Ontario.

Your medical practitioner or optometrist is required by law to report to the licensing authorities any physical, neurological, cardio-vascular or other medical condition that might affect your safe operation of a motor vehicle.

Your application will be refused if your physical or medical condition does not meet the standards outlined in the regulations of the *Highway Traffic Act*.

Knowledge test checklist

Before taking the class A or D knowledge test, make sure you have studied the *Official MTO Truck Handbook*.
Bring the following items to the test:

- Two pieces of identification or Ontario driver's licence
- Complete medical report form
- Money for test fees – cash, debit or credit card
- Glasses or contact lenses (if you need to wear them to read or write)

Class A or D road test

All road tests have a set time frame. Before you begin your test, the examiner will inform you of the amount of time you have to complete each part of the test. The examiner will explain the test, and you are to follow her or his instructions. The examiner is not allowed to coach you during the test so, if you have any questions, ask them before you begin. On the road test:

- You will be required to demonstrate a daily inspection (See pages 19 to 21.) You will be required to name the item of equipment checked and briefly describe its condition.
- Class A applicants will demonstrate uncoupling and coupling of the units of the combination vehicle.
- Class A applicants will demonstrate backing (reversing) of the units of the combination vehicle.
- Applicants will be required to drive in traffic and handle the vehicle safely.

Class A or D road test checklist

- Study the *Official MTO Truck Handbook* before the test.
- Study the operating manual for the vehicle to be used for the road test.
- Bring the appropriate type of vehicle, in good working order, to the test.
- Bring glasses or contact lenses if you need to wear them to drive. (If your current licence is conditional on wearing corrective lenses, you cannot drive without wearing them.)
- Bring wheel chocks or blocks, if the vehicle is equipped with air brakes.

Commercial Vehicle Operator Registration (CVOR)

CVOR is the registration system that tracks the safety performance of truck and bus operations in Ontario.

A commercial vehicle operator is a person or company that is responsible for the operation of a truck or bus, including the conduct of the driver, mechanical condition of the vehicle and the safe transportation of goods or passengers.

A CVOR certificate is required to operate trucks having a registered plated weight (or actual weight) over 4,500 kilograms (9,920 lbs) and buses designed to carry 10 or more passengers. This rule applies to vehicles that are plated in Ontario, the United States or Mexico and that travel in Ontario.

To register for a CVOR certificate a carrier must complete a "Commercial Vehicle Operator's Registration" certificate application.

A fee of $250 will apply for the application and issuance of an original CVOR certificate.

Commercial vehicles exceptions

- Ambulances
- Fire department vehicles
- Hearses and casket wagons
- Motor homes

Personal use exemptions

- Buses that are used for personal purposes
- Commercial motor vehicles leased for no longer than 30 days for personal use by an individual (for example, moving own household goods) or used for the transportation of passengers without compensation
- Most pick-up trucks being used for personal purposes (without compensation) and not carrying, or towing a trailer that is carrying cargo or tools or equipment normally used for commercial purposes

Permit exemptions

- Commercial motor vehicles operating under the authority of an In-Transit permit
- Temporary permits and number plates in the possession of vehicle manufacturers, vehicles dealers, or businesses that repair, road test, customize or modify vehicles

The CVOR record contains information that includes:

- Carrier information (kilometric travel, violation rates, safety rating)
- Reportable collisions
- Convictions that are entered against the operator and/or any driver who operates under your CVOR certificate
- All inspections of the operator's fleet, with or without defects

All items remain on the operator's CVOR record for a period of five years from the date of the offence.

If an operator's record becomes unacceptable, the ministry may send a warning letter to the operator, conduct an audit or request that the operator attend a meeting to discuss the record. If the operator's record does not improve, the ministry may impose sanctions, including the cancellation or suspension of the CVOR certificate, plates and permits.

Size and weight limits for commercial motor vehicles

Commercial motor vehicles are restricted in width to a limit of 2.6 metres (8.5 ft.). Exceptions are made for specialized equipment such as snow removal equipment. In determining the width of a motor vehicle, the mirrors will not be included if they do not extend more than 30 centimetres beyond the vehicle on either side. In regards to the width of a motor vehicle or trailer equipped with auxiliary equipment, it will not be included in the width, provided it does not extend more than 10 centimetres from the side of the vehicle and is not designed or used to carry a load. Semi-trailers are limited to a length of 14.65 metres (48 ft.) or 16.2 metres (53 ft.) if the trailer and tractor meet special requirements.

No combination of vehicles is permitted to exceed a length of 23 metres (75.5 ft.) except double-trailer combinations that meet special requirements for both trailers and the tractor.

Diagram 1-2

All vehicles, including loads are limited to a height of 4.15 metres (13.6 ft.) to ensure adequate clearance is maintained at bridges and overpasses.

You cannot operate a vehicle or combination of vehicles on a highway when its gross weight exceeds the maximum weight permitted under Part VII of the *Highway Traffic Act* and its regulations.

To determine the gross allowable weight of a commercial vehicle, several factors must be considered, including the number of axles, the size of the tires, the type of suspension, the distance between the axles, the type of load carried (aggregate or non-aggregate load) and the weight allowed on the steering axle.

Several formulas are used to determine the maximum allowable gross weight. These include calculating the sum of the weights allowed on each axle, the registered gross vehicle weight or the weight prescribed in regulations under the *Highway Traffic Act*. Once these weights have been determined, the lower figure of these is the maximum gross allowable weight.

Drivers, operators and shippers are all responsible for the weight of the commercial vehicle, and any may be charged with an offence.

IV. VEHICLE SAFETY, MAINTENANCE AND DAILY INSPECTIONS

Ministry of Transportation inspection stations

The Ministry of Transportation monitors the condition of commercial motor vehicles operating in Ontario and, when necessary, takes corrective action. One method of accomplishing this task is through vehicle inspections, which can be performed by ministry enforcement staff or police officers. Ministry enforcement staff perform inspections at truck inspection stations.

Truck inspection stations are found at various highway locations in Ontario. Signs indicate whether or not a station is open. If a station is open, trucks must enter and stop for inspection.

Vehicles and loads are checked for weight, height, length, width and axle spacing. Driver licences are also checked for validity and proper class of licence for the vehicle.

All drivers of a commercial vehicle as defined in Regulation 419/15 (Definitions of Commercial Motor Vehicle and Tow Truck) of the *Highway Traffic Act* should carry and surrender on demand the following documents:

- A valid driver's licence of the appropriate class for the vehicle being operated
- The registration or a true copy for the truck and trailer (if any) being operated
- The CVOR certificate or true copy of the individual or company responsible for the driver, vehicle and its load
- An original insurance certificate for the vehicle being operated (vehicle-specific or a fleet policy)
- A daily inspection report that has been completed within 24 hours and a copy of the appropriate inspection schedule

- A daily log for the day and the previous fourteen days
- All supporting documents to the driver, including but not limited to fuel, bridge, toll and accommodation receipts

If a driver is directed to operate within a 160-km radius of where they start the day and return to the same location at the end of the day, they may be exempt from carrying a daily log, but will still be subject to all of the requirements for hours of service.

Vehicles are subject to safety checks (for example, of brakes, lights, couplings). In addition to permanent truck-inspection stations, mobile-inspection units may be set up for varying lengths of time at any location.

Any police officer or appointed ministry officer has the authority to perform a safety inspection at any time and any location. They may require you to drive to the nearest

inspection station. If requested, you must assist in the inspection of the vehicle. Inspections may be done on a highway at any time.

If you refuse or fail to proceed to a weigh scale when requested, you are guilty of an offence and liable to a fine of up to $20,000 under section 124(5) of the *HTA*. You may also have your licence suspended for up to 30 days.

Drivers who refuse or fail to redistribute or remove part of a load, or make arrangements to do so, or obstruct a weighing, measuring or examination, are guilty of an offence and liable to a fine of $200 to $20,000 under section 124(6) of the *HTA*.

Tires and wheels

Another important component of vehicle safety is tires and wheels. You must check the tires and wheels of your vehicle as part of the pre-trip inspection to ensure they meet safety standards. For example, you must check your tires to ensure they have appropriate tread depth; and check your wheels to ensure they are securely attached. The rear tire of a motor vehicle must not have less than 1.5 millimetres (0.06 in.) of tread measured in two adjacent tread grooves. The front tires of a motor vehicle with a gross vehicle rating of more than 4,500 kilograms must have at least 3 millimetres (0.12 in.) of tread measured in two adjacent tread grooves.

It is also a good safety practice to inspect the wheels, wheel fasteners and tires after having new tires or wheels installed, or if the wheels have been removed for repairs to other components. Wheel manufacturers recommend having wheel fasteners re-checked between 80 km and 160 km after installation. Wheels and tires must be installed by a certified tire installer or a mechanic.

Steering

Free play or lash in the steering system is the distance the steering wheel moves before the tires begin turning. Check with the engine on and the wheels straight ahead; turn the steering wheel in both directions with your fingers until you can feel the resistance of the tires. If the steering wheel rotates too far, there is excessive free play or lash in the steering system.

Cargo securement

As the driver, you are responsible for making sure the cargo is evenly balanced and properly secured against shifting. Any cargo that breaks loose or shifts could cause a collision or vehicle rollover. All loads carried on a motor vehicle or trailer must be bound, covered or otherwise securely fastened or loaded such that no portion of the load can fall off the vehicle or trailer. (See Diagram 1-3.)

Diagram 1-3

The *Highway Traffic Act* states that any load overhanging the rear of a vehicle by 1.5 metres (5 ft.) or more should be marked by a red light when lights are required (one-half hour before sunset to one-half hour after sunrise or at other times of poor light conditions) and, at all other times, by a red flag or red marker.

Before driving with a load, you should know the type of cargo you are carrying and the required means of securing the load to the vehicle. Many commodities require safety devices for the driver such as protective bulkheads or special lading. Before starting any trip, check that doors are latched or that racks, tarps and other equipment are properly secured.

The vehicle's cargo must be inspected to ensure it is secure before driving the vehicle. Re-check it not more than 80 km from the point where the cargo was loaded.

The driver shall re-inspect the vehicle's cargo and the cargo securement systems, and make adjustments at intervals, based on whichever of the following occurs first:
- There is a change of duty status of the driver.
- The vehicle has been driven for three hours.
- The vehicle has been driven for 240 km.

Note: The driver is not required to inspect the load when the cargo is sealed in a vehicle and the driver has been ordered not to open it, or if the cargo is inaccessible.

Ontario has adopted National Safety Code (NSC) Standard 10 for Cargo Securement, developed and published by the Canadian Council for Motor Transport Administrators (CCMTA). Standard 10 provides detailed instructions for operators and drivers to follow when securing different types of loads to commercial vehicles. Every commercial vehicle carrying cargo on Ontario's roads must comply with the rules set out for cargo securement in this national standard. The standard was developed to increase both public safety and the safety of commercial vehicle drivers carrying loads. To read NSC Standard 10 for Cargo Securement, visit CCMTA's website at www.ccmta.ca. See also Ontario Regulation 363/04 "Security of Loads" in the *Highway Traffic Act* at www.e-laws.gov.on.ca.

Annual inspection certificate

Operators are responsible for having each of their vehicles and trailers inspected each year by a licensed motor-vehicle inspection mechanic. The mechanic checks to ensure that the vehicle or trailer is in compliance with all of the inspection requirements contained in the appropriate standard of the National Safety Code 11, Part B. To read NSC standard 11 for Periodic Commercial Motor Vehicle Maintenance Inspections (PMVI) standards, visit CCMTA's website at www.ccmta.ca. This standard has been adopted through regulation under the *Highway Traffic Act*.

If the vehicle/trailer is in compliance with all requirements, the mechanic or another person authorized by the inspection station completes an annual inspection certificate and an annual inspection record. These documents come with a corresponding annual inspection sticker (decal), which indicates the vehicle type, as well as the month and year of the inspection. The mechanic or other authorized person places the decal on the outside lower left corner of the windshield or left side of the truck cab, or on the outside surface on the front left side of a trailer, semi-trailer or trailer converter dolly.

Drivers are also responsible for ensuring the vehicle they are driving is fit for highway use. As part of your daily inspection, check the date on the inspection-certificate decal on the vehicle and/or trailer to ensure that it is still valid.

V. DAILY INSPECTION -CLASSES A AND D

Drivers play an important part in making sure that trucks using Ontario highways are in good operating condition. The most effective method for drivers to determine that their vehicle is in safe operating condition is to do a daily inspection before starting the day's trip. To assist you in performing the daily inspection, you must use the applicable schedule. You may also follow a systematic approach or inspection sheet.

Not only is it good safety practice, the daily inspection is a requirement of the *Highway Traffic Act*. Drivers must, by law, inspect their vehicles and be capable of determining if they are in a safe operating condition. A driver is required to complete a vehicle inspection, which will be valid for a 24-hour period.

A driver is not permitted to drive a truck unless they or another person, within the previous 24 hours, have conducted a daily inspection

Diagram 1-4

according to Schedule 1 inspection and sign a completed inspection report. If the driver is not the person who conducted the daily inspection for the vehicle or trailer, the driver is responsible to sign a completed daily inspection report before operating the vehicle.

The inspection is conducted in accordance with an inspection schedule. The schedule provides a list of vehicle systems and components that a driver is required to inspect, and provides a list of defects to guide and assist the driver.

The inspection schedule divides defects into two categories: major and minor. A major defect such as a flat tire and broken main leaf spring pose immediate safety risks, while minor defects may be less urgent (for example, broken clearance lamps and damaged wiper blade). When a defect is identified, the driver must record the defect on the daily inspection report, inform the operator and

monitor the condition. Drivers are not permitted to operate a vehicle with a major defect.

A completed, signed daily inspection report is required even when no defect is found. A driver picking up a trailer at another location must complete a separate daily inspection report for that trailer. Drivers must carry both current inspection report and the inspection schedule at all times. Electronic reports and schedules are permitted.

The daily inspection in this book shows the absolute minimum inspection that must be performed. For the full inspection schedules outlining all major and minor defects, which all commercial vehicle drivers are required to complete daily, refer to the Ontario Regulation 199/07 "Commercial Motor Vehicle Inspections" in the *Highway Traffic Act* at www.e-laws.gov.on.ca. For additional information on how

to perform a daily inspection in accordance with Regulation 199/07, go to www.ontario.ca and type the following information into the search box: "Trucks and Buses, Commercial Vehicle Operators' Safety Manual". On the Trucks and Buses page, type "Module 8" in the search box.

In cases where serious infractions are discovered, the vehicle is taken out of service. For less serious infractions, such as broken clearance lamps, drivers must report the condition to the operator so that repairs can be made in a timely manner.

It is very important that drivers also complete a proper air brake pre-trip inspection as described in The *Official MTO Air Brake Handbook* before starting the day's trip. The driver must ensure at all times that the brakes on the vehicle are not out-of-adjustment.

Note: You cannot adjust your own air brakes unless you have either completed an approved air brake adjustment course or you are a certified mechanic.

Daily inspection

Details of the inspection can change according to the type of vehicle, but generally the principle of making a complete inspection should be followed.

As part of the daily inspection, you must inspect all items according to the applicable schedule in Ontario Regulation 199/07. The daily inspection must include the following items:

- Air brake system (if equipped)
- Cab
- Cargo securement (if present)
- Coupling devices (if equipped)
- Dangerous goods (for qualified driver only)
- Driver controls
- Driver seat
- Electric brake system
- Emergency equipment and safety devices
- Exhaust system
- Frame and cargo body
- Fuel system
- Glass and mirrors
- Heater / Defroster
- Horn
- Hydraulic brake system
- Lamp and reflectors
- Steering
- Suspension system
- Tires
- Wheels, hub, and fasteners
- Windshield wiper / washer

For examination process, refer to The Road Test, page 113.

Uncoupling and coupling of combinations (Class A only)

Knowing how to couple and uncouple correctly is basic to safe operation of combination vehicles; incorrect uncoupling and coupling can be very dangerous. There are differences between different trucks and trailers, so make sure you learn the details of coupling and uncoupling the truck(s) and trailer(s) you will operate.

Prior to uncoupling/coupling procedure you must always remember:

- Roll down windows and turn off any audio systems.
- Sound your horn before backing (electric horn only if during the road test).
- Confirm the location is suitable and safe for uncoupling and coupling the truck and trailer.

Uncoupling

1. Secure truck/tractor and trailer.

- Ensure both truck/tractor and trailer parking brakes are applied.
- Place transmission in park/neutral.
- Ensure trailer wheels are chocked properly.

2. Lower landing gear.

- Check to see if the ground is level and secure.
- Lower the landing gear until it is:
  I. Just above the ground or,
  II. Makes contact with the ground, but does not raise the trailer from the fifth wheel and ensure there is no gap between trailer and fifth wheel.

- Stow the landing-gear handle (fifth wheel) in low gear.

3. Disconnect and stow air and electrical lines, safety chains or cables.

- Disconnect and secure air and electrical lines (if equipped).
- Disconnect and secure safety chains or cables (if equipped).

4. Unlock fifth wheel / unlatch coupling device.

- Unlock fifth wheel or coupling device.

Non-fifth wheel:

- Raise the trailer until the trailer coupling device clears the truck coupling device.
- Confirm the trailer is stable and secure.
- Stow the landing gear handle (non-fifth wheel).

Note: Steps 3 and 4 may be completed in either order. For non-fifth wheel tractor trailer vehicles, pull the truck clear of the trailer by releasing the truck parking brake and pull ahead slowly until the two units are separated.

5. Disengage fifth wheel (fifth wheel tractor trailer only).

- Pull the tractor forward far enough to disengage the fifth wheel.
- Ensure the fifth wheel is not in contact with the trailer, and the tractor frame is still under the trailer.
- Apply tractor parking brakes and place transmission in neutral.

6. Confirm trailer is stable (fifth wheel tractor trailer only).

- Exit the vehicle to confirm trailer is stable and secure.

7. Pull tractor clear of trailer (fifth wheel tractor trailer only).

- Release tractor parking brakes and pull ahead slowly until the two units are separated.

Coupling

1. Inspect fifth wheel, coupling device, air/electrical lines, chain hook points and connections.

Fifth wheel:

- Inspect fifth wheel, air/electrical lines and connections.

Non-fifth wheel:

- Inspect truck coupling device, truck air/electrical connections and chain connection points as applicable.

2. Position truck/tractor and trailer units. Check trailer alignment and height.

- Before reversing, exit vehicle (if required), check vehicle path and observe environment around the vehicle, activate four-way flashers and sound horn. (If vehicle is equipped with an automatic audible backing device, sounding horn is not required).
- Reverse the truck/tractor slowly at a walking pace.

Fifth wheel:

- Reverse until the fifth wheel is just ahead of trailer, touching the trailer or slightly under, but not against the kingpin.

Non-fifth wheel:

- Reverse until the truck coupling device is one foot ahead of trailer connection point (touching the trailer is acceptable however

moving the wheel chocks is not acceptable).
- Place transmission in park/neutral and apply truck/tractor parking brakes.

Fifth wheel:
- Inspect trailer upper coupler plate and kingpin or trailer connection points.
- Inspect trailer air and electrical lines and connections.
- Confirm the kingpin is aligned with the fifth wheel lower coupler.

Non-fifth wheel:
- Confirm the truck coupling device and trailer connection point is aligned.
- Confirm the trailer height is correct.
- Adjust truck/tractor position, alignment or trailer height if necessary.

Note: The trailer should be low enough that it is raised slightly by the tractor when the tractor is backed under it. Raise or lower the trailer as needed. (If the trailer is too low, the tractor may strike and damage the trailer nose; if the trailer is too high, it may not couple correctly).

3. Engage fifth wheel and test or engage truck coupling device and trailer connection point.

Fifth wheel:
- Reverse the tractor, properly engaging the fifth wheel.
- Perform tug test by stretching the tractor and trailer to confirm the trailer is locked onto the tractor.
- Apply tractor parking brakes and place transmission in neutral.

Non-fifth wheel:
- Reverse the truck until coupling device is properly in-line with the trailer connection point.
- Place transmission in park/neutral and apply truck parking brake.
- Adjust landing gear or trailer position/height as necessary to complete coupling.
- Connect the safety chains or cables crossed.

4. Confirm fifth-wheel lock or coupling device locked.

Exit tractor and visually confirm:
Fifth wheel:

- There is no space above fifth wheel. (If any space appears between the upper plate of the trailer and fifth wheel, this indicates that the coupling is not secure.)
- The release lever is in the locked position.
- The fifth-wheel jaws or locking lever/latch has closed around the kingpin (applicant must get under trailer).

Non-fifth wheel:
- Ensure coupling device is locked, secondary locks are secured, and connection points, chains and hooks are properly connected.

5. Connect air and electrical lines.
- Properly connect air and electrical line(s) (if equipped).
- Connect breakaway device if equipped.

Note: Industry standard colours are:
BLUE - service
RED - supply or emergency

6. Raise the trailer landing gear.
- Raise the trailer landing gear fully.
- Stow the handle into its retainer.

7. Supply air to trailer.
- Supply air to the trailer with the trailer supply valve and establish normal air pressure.
- Shut off the engine and from the cab:
  - **I.** Listen for leakage from the supply connection.
  - **II.** Apply service brakes and listen for leakage from service connection.

8. Test brake operation.
- Drive forward slowly and test brake operation as soon as possible.

To test hook-up
Place the transmission in reverse and then partially release the clutch to move the power unit backward in a short, sharp motion. This is known as "hitting the pin."

Depress the clutch and place the transmission in the lowest forward gear. If the vehicle is equipped with a trailer hand control, pull it down to set trailer brakes to keep the unit from rolling. If there is no hand control, set the trailer parking brake.

Try to pull forward against the pin.

Check coupling (visual inspection)
- Leave the cab and look under the front of the trailer to be sure that its upper plate is resting firmly on the fifth wheel. If any space appears, the coupling is not secure.
- Be sure the fifth-wheel release lever is in locked position and the secondary lock, if there is one, is engaged.
- From behind the tractor and under the trailer, see that the jaws are completely closed.

Raise the landing gear after checking the hook-up and before moving the unit. Be sure the gear is fully raised.

If you use a two-speed crank gear, place it in low range, and stow the crank securely.

VI. COMMERCIAL VEHICLE IMPOUNDMENT PROGRAM

Under Ontario Regulation 512/97, the Registrar of Motor Vehicles may impound a commercial vehicle found with critical defects. Critical defects are defined in Ontario Regulation 512/97 for brakes (air and hydraulic), steering, wheels and rims, tires and frame and suspension. The impound period for a vehicle found to be operating with critical defects at a commercial vehicle impound program inspection station is 15 days for the first offence. If the same vehicle turns up with critical defects within a two-year timeframe, the impoundment period doubles to 30 days. A third or subsequent offence within the same two years will result in an impoundment period of 60 days.

The fines for driving a vehicle with critical defects can be up to $20,000. Impoundment affects commercial vehicles as defined in Regulation 419/15 (Definitions of Commercial Motor Vehicle and Tow Truck) of the *HTA* only.

VII. HOURS OF SERVICE

This section provides an overview of the basic rules. All the details of the hours-of-service requirements are contained in the *Highway Traffic Act* in Ontario Regulation 555/06.

Drivers required to comply with hours-of-service regulations

The hours-of-service regulations apply to drivers of the following types of vehicles:
- Commercial motor vehicles having gross weight or registered gross weight over 4,500 kilograms
- Buses, school buses and school-purposes buses

Exemptions to hours-of-service regulations

Drivers of the following types of vehicles are not required to comply with the hours-of-service regulations:
- Commercial motor vehicles, other than buses, having gross weight or registered gross weight of not more than 4,500 kilograms
- Commercial motor vehicles leased for no longer than 30 days by an individual
- Commercial motor vehicles, operated under dealer or service permits, that are not transporting passengers or goods
- Two- or three-axle commercial motor vehicles transporting primary farm, forest, sea or lake products
- Pick-up trucks, being used for personal purposes, that have a manufacturer's gross vehicle weight rating of 6,000 kilograms or less

- Tow trucks
- Motor homes
- Municipal buses operated as part of a public transit service
- Buses used for personal purposes without compensation
- Vehicles being used by a police officers
- Cardiac arrest vehicles
- Vehicles engaged in providing relief in emergencies
- Ambulances, fire apparatus, hearses or casket wagon

Duty status

The rules define four categories of duty time for commercial vehicle drivers:
1. Off-duty time, other than time spent in a sleeper berth
2. Off-duty time spent in a sleeper berth
3. On-duty time spent driving
4. On-duty time, other than time spent driving

On-duty activities include driving, as well as performing any other activities for the operator, such as inspecting, cleaning or repairing your vehicle; travelling as a co-driver (not including when in sleeper berth); loading and unloading the vehicle; waiting at inspections for unloading or loading to be completed, or because of an unforeseen occurrence such as an accident.

These four categories are used to determine the minimum off-duty required and the maximum on-duty times allowed for commercial vehicle drivers.

Hours-of-service requirements
1. Daily requirement*
- A driver must have 10 hours off-duty in a day.
- A driver cannot drive more than 13 hours in a day.
- A driver cannot drive after 14 hours on-duty in a day.
* Some exceptions apply; refer to Ontario Regulation 555/06

2. Mandatory off-duty time
- After a period of at least eight hours off-duty, a driver cannot drive more than 13 hours.
- After a period of at least eight hours off-duty, a driver cannot drive after having been on-duty for 14 hours.
- After a period of at least eight hours off-duty, a driver cannot drive after 16 hours has elapsed.

3. Cycle requirement
- An operator shall designate a cycle for the driver to follow.
- There are two cycles available, a seven-day cycle or a 14-day cycle.
- In a period of seven consecutive days, a driver cannot drive after having been on-duty for 70 hours.
- In a period of 14 consecutive days, a driver cannot drive after having been on-duty for 120 hours. Drivers following this cycle shall not drive after accumulating 70 hours on-duty without having taken 24 consecutive hours of off-duty time.
- On any day, all drivers must have a period of at least 24 consecutive hours off-duty in the preceding 14 days.

4. Cycle reset/switching
- A driver may only switch the cycle they are on if they start a new cycle.
- To start a new cycle, a driver on the seven-day cycle must take 36 consecutive hours off-duty.
- To start a new cycle, a driver on the 14-day cycle must take 72 consecutive hours off-duty.

5. Daily log requirement
A daily log may be handwritten, computer generated or made by means of a recording device. The daily log must contain the following information:

- Driver's name
- Date
- Name of the driver's co-drivers, if any
- Start time of the day being recorded, if the day does not start at midnight
- Cycle that the driver is following
- Odometer reading, at the start of the day
- Number plate of each commercial motor vehicle to be driven and each trailer
- Name of the operator
- Address of the driver's home terminal and of the principal place of business of the operator
- Graph grid as illustrated in Form 1 of the regulation (not required for Recording Device)
- Start and end times for each duty status during the day
- Location where the driver's duty status changes
- Total time spent in each duty status during the day

- Odometer reading at the end of the day
- Total distance driven by the driver
- Driver's signature

6. Daily log exemption

A driver is not required to keep a daily log if the driver:
- Drives the commercial motor vehicle solely within a radius of 160 kilometres of the location at which the driver starts the day
- Returns at the end of the day to the same location from which he or she started
- Only works for one operator that day

If a driver is not required to keep a daily log, the operator shall keep a record for the day showing:
- Date, driver's name and the location where the driver starts and ends the day

- Cycle that the driver is following
- Hour at which each duty status starts and ends
- Total number of hours spent in each duty status

These rules will help keep Ontario's roads safe by allowing commercial drivers to get the rest they need in order to safely operate their vehicles. For more details about the hours-of-service requirements, visit the MTO website at www.mto.gov.on.ca, or refer to the *Highway Traffic Act* at www.e-laws.gov.on.ca.

Chapter 1-Summary

By the end of this chapter you should know:

- The different licence classifications and what types of vehicles they permit you to drive
- The requirements you must meet to obtain a truck driver's licence
- The requirements for Commercial Vehicle Operator Registration (CVOR) and vehicle documentation
- The size and weight limits for commercial motor vehicles
- The requirements for truck inspections, vehicle maintenance and inspection stations
- The requirements for vehicle loads and load security
- The requirements for daily inspection
- The hours-of-service requirements for all commercial vehicle drivers

CHAPTER 2
DRIVING—CLASSES A AND D

Starting the engine
1. Engage the parking brake, depress the clutch pedal and place the transmission in neutral.
2. Turn on the power to the engine; operate the starter.
3. If necessary, increase engine speed with the accelerator pedal until it is running smoothly.
4. Check the gauge for adequate engine oil pressure.
5. On vehicles with air brakes, the air-pressure gauge should register sufficient pressure before moving. The audible air warning buzzer must have stopped sounding and/or the warning light must be off.

Note: For more information on air brakes, see The Offiřial MTO Air Brake Handbook.

Putting vehicle into motion
When starting to move, gradually release the clutch and at the same time release the hand control valve or parking brake. At the same time, the engine must be speeded up gradually on some vehicles to prevent stalling. Check the brakes immediately after you have the vehicle underway, within at least 15 metres (50 ft.).

Transmissions
- It is your responsibility to be thoroughly familiar with trans-mission shift patterns and shifting procedures. We recommend that you study the truck manufacturer's operating manual.
- When you start to move, put the vehicle in the lowest appropriate gear.

- Do not shock-load the drive line by abruptly releasing the clutch pedal. Apply power gradually when moving heavy loads uphill.
- Do not allow the clutch to slip excessively, since this can overheat the clutch and cause damage.

Remember: Co-ordinated clutch operation and smooth transmission shifting will prolong the life of any vehicle.

Some vehicles are equipped with a clutch brake. When driving them, the clutch pedal should not be depressed all the way to the floor when shifting, except at a stop. To re-enter low gear, depress the pedal to the floor to produce an easy, quiet engagement into low gear, with the vehicle at rest.

Inter-axle differential lock

The inter-axle differential lock is used on vehicles with tandem rear axles.

Differential lock is controlled by a lever or push-pull control valve on the instrument panel.

This feature can be in only two positions–lock or unlock– as indicated.

Periodically, the valve should be operated to make sure it moves freely; normally the valve should be kept in the unlock position.

Use the lock position only when you approach conditions where one or both wheels of an axle may slip. The valve locks the differential and causes it to act as a "through drive," transmitting power equally to both axles. Avoid unnecessary use of differential lock since it will result in tire wear and axle strain.

Caution: You should not activate the differential lock when the wheels are actually spinning.

Note: Proper operating instructions vary from manufacturer to manufacturer. Refer to your owner's manual for further instructions.

Brake inspection

While the drivers are not expected to be able to service a disabled braking system, you should be knowledgeable enough to identify if the brakes are not performing properly.

1. **Hydraulic brakes** (with power assist):
   - With the engine stopped, pump the brake pedal several times to eliminate power assist.
   - Apply brakes moderately.
   - Start the engine (the pedal should drop slightly and stop).
   - If the pedal continues to drop or does not drop (no power assist) stop the engine. The vehicle should be taken out of service and the system inspected professionally.
2. **Hydraulic brakes** (without power assist):
   - Apply brakes moderately and hold.
   - If the pedal shows a steady drop, the vehicle should be

taken out of service and the system inspected professionally.

Use of brakes

Apply steady pressure at the beginning of a stop, then ease off as the vehicle slows. Just before the vehicle comes to a complete stop, release the brakes enough to avoid a jerk and rebound, then apply the brakes again to hold the vehicle while stopped. For details on the use of Hydraulics and Anti Lock Braking Systems (ABS), see page 55.

You should not fan your brakes (alternately apply and release them) except on slippery pavement where this type of braking (also called threshold braking) gives better control, reduces danger of skidding and gives a shorter stop. Fanning reduces air pressure and serves no useful purpose on dry pavement, and fanning on a long downhill grade may reduce air pressure below the minimum pressure needed for proper brake operation.

Take great care to avoid excessive use of brakes on long downgrades, as overheated brakes are dangerously inefficient. Use engine braking as the principal means of controlling speed on long grades. If possible, you should use the same gear in descending a long grade as you would climbing it. Make your gear selection before descending a grade to minimize the chance of missing a shift.

If the low air-pressure warning device operates at anytime, stop immediately in the safest available place and correct the loss of air pressure before proceeding.

If brakes should fail on a level road, you should downshift and use engine braking to slow the vehicle. If a shorter stopping distance is necessary, use the tractor and trailer emergency brakes, if fitted, to stop. You should not drive the vehicle again until repairs have been made.

In a combination of vehicles such as a truck-tractor and semi-trailer, trailer brakes are applied with the truck brakes using the foot control valve. This is known as balanced braking. The pressure applied on both the trailer and the truck-tractor brakes is the same. Trailer brakes may be applied independently by using the trailer hand valve. Pulling harder on the hand valve may increase the amount of pressure on the trailer brakes during a foot valve application.

Exercise care in braking a combination of vehicles on wet or slippery surfaces, or on a curve. Over-braking in these circumstances can result in skidding or jackknifing. If the tractor is jackknifing (if the tractor rear wheels slide sideways) apply the trailer brakes only. If the trailer rear wheels slide sideways, release all brakes and gradually apply the accelerator.

Spring brakes are designed to work when you are parking your vehicle or in an emergency when your service brakes fail. They apply automatically when the air pressure in the system drops below a predetermined level (normally 414 kPa or 60 psi).

Note: If you plan to operate a vehicle equipped with air brakes, refer to The **Offifial MTO Air Brake Handbook** for further information.

Note: Some municipalities may have restrictions on engine braking. Ensure that you follow the restriction signs in each municipality.

Parking

To ensure that a unit will stay in position when parked, take the following precautions:

1. Set parking brakes.
2. Block the unit by placing chocks or blocks on the rear wheel (front and back of wheel) on one or both sides of the unit or trailer.
3. Under no circumstances should a driver use the trailer hand valve, or the tractor protection valve to hold a parked unit.

Stopping

Knowing how to stop safely and properly is an important driving skill. Safe and responsible drivers see stops ahead, check their mirrors, begin braking early and stop smoothly. Braking is easier when you sit properly. Use your right foot for both brake and accelerator pedals so you won't step on both pedals at the same time or activate your brake lights unnecessarily. Press the brake pedal firmly and evenly.

Shift into a lower gear when going down long, steep hills. This will help control your speed and you won't have to brake as sharply.

Diagram 2-1

Diagram 2-2

Downshift before starting downhill since it may not be possible once you are going downhill. As a guide, you should be in the same gear going downhill as uphill. When climbing a steep hill and your speed is reduced, you should continue driving and activate your four-way flashers throughout the ascent.

You must come to a complete stop for all stop signs and red traffic lights. Stop at the stop line if it is marked on the pavement. If there is no stop line, stop at the crosswalk, marked or not. If there is no crosswalk, stop at the edge of the sidewalk. If there is no sidewalk, stop at the edge of the intersection (Diagram 2-2). Wait until the way is clear before entering the intersection.

Stopping at railway crossings

All railway crossings on public roads in Ontario are marked with large red and white 'X' signs. Watch for these signs and be prepared to stop. You may also see yellow advance warning signs and large 'X' pavement markings ahead of railway crossings. Some railway crossings have flashing

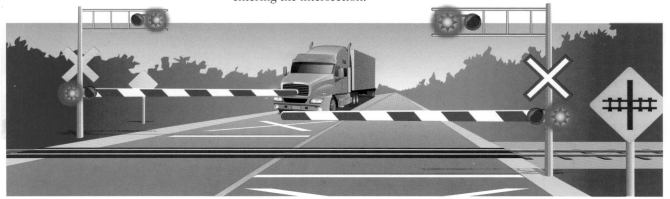

Diagram 2-3

signal lights and some use gates or barriers to keep drivers from crossing the tracks when a train is coming. Some less-travelled crossings have stop signs posted. Remember, it can take up to two kilometres for a train to stop under full emergency braking. On private roads, railway crossings may not be marked, so watch carefully. When you come to a railway crossing, remember:

- Slow down, listen and look both ways to make sure the way is clear before crossing the tracks.
- If a train is coming, stop at least five metres from the nearest rail or gate. Do not cross the track until you are sure the train or trains have passed.
- Never race a train to a crossing.
- If there are signal lights, wait until they stop flashing and, if the crossing has a gate or barrier, wait until it rises, before you cross the tracks.
- Never drive around, under or through a railway gate or barrier while it is down, being lowered or being raised. It is illegal and dangerous.
- Avoid stopping in the middle of railway tracks; for example, in heavy traffic, make sure you have enough room to cross the tracks completely before you begin to cross.
- Avoid shifting gears while crossing tracks.
- If you get trapped on a crossing, immediately get everyone out and away from the vehicle. Move to a safe place and then contact authorities.
- Buses and other public vehicles are required to stop at railway crossings that are not protected by gates, signal lights or a stop sign. School buses must stop at railway crossings whether or not they are protected by gates or signal lights. Watch for these buses and be prepared to stop behind them.

If you are approaching a railway crossing with a stop sign, you must stop unless otherwise directed by a flagman.

Stopping at school crossings

Where a school-crossing guard displays a red and white stop sign, you must stop before reaching the crossing and remain stopped until all people, including the school crossing guard, have cleared the entire roadway and it is safe to proceed. If you have any doubts

Diagram 2-4

Diagram 2-5

about when it is safe to drive forward, wait until all the children and the guard have cleared the crossing. Drivers who don't follow the stopping requirements may receive a substantial fine and get three demerit points.

Stopping for school buses

School buses in Ontario come in a range of sizes. All are chrome yellow and display the words "School Bus."

You must stop whenever you approach a stopped school bus with its upper alternating red lights flashing, regardless of whether you are behind the bus or approaching it from the front. When approaching the bus from the front, stop at a safe distance for children to get off the bus and cross the road in front of you. If you are coming from behind the bus, stop at least 20 metres away. Do not go until the bus moves or the lights have stopped flashing.

If you are on a road with a median strip, only vehicles coming from behind the bus must stop. (A median is a physical barrier such as a raised, lowered, earth or paved strip constructed to separate traffic travelling in different directions. Vehicles cannot cross over a median strip.)

You must obey the school bus law on any road, no matter how many lanes or what the speed limit. Be prepared to stop for a school bus at any time, not just within school hours.

As well as the upper alternating red flashing lights, school buses use a stop-sign arm on the driver's side of the bus. This arm, a standard stop sign with alternating flashing red lights at top and bottom, swings out after the upper alternating red lights begin to flash. Remain stopped until the arm folds away and all lights stop flashing.

It is illegal to fail to stop for a stopped school bus that has its red lights flashing. If you don't stop, you can be fined $400 to $2,000 and receive six demerit points for a first offence. If you are convicted a second time within five years, the penalty is a fine of $1,000 to $4,000 and six demerit points. You could also go to jail for up to six months. In Ontario, school bus drivers and other witnesses can report vehicles that have illegally passed a school bus.

As the vehicle's registered owner, you may receive the fines if the driver is not charged. If you do not pay the fine, you will not be able to renew your vehicle permit.

Note: Watch for school buses near railway crossings. All school buses must stop at all railway crossings; however, the upper alternating red lights are not used for these stops.

Stopping for pedestrian crossovers

Pedestrian crossovers (commonly called crosswalks) are designated areas that allow pedestrians to safely cross roads where there are no traffic lights. Always watch for pedestrians and people using wheelchairs at these crossings. Pedestrians may push a button to make overhead yellow lights flash to warn drivers. Pedestrians should point across the road to show they want to cross before entering the roadway. Drivers, including cyclists, must stop and allow pedestrians to cross. Once people have cleared your side of the road, you can proceed with

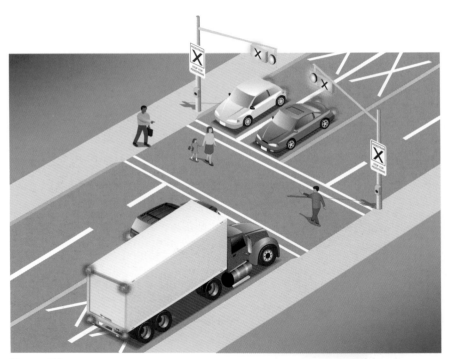

Diagram 2-6

caution. Do not pass any vehicle within 30 metres of a pedestrian crossover. Never pass a vehicle that has stopped to allow pedestrians to cross the road.

Clearances

When you drive a larger vehicle, you must know the vehicle's height and width, and watch for and obey clearance signs on bridges and underpasses. The maximum height for a vehicle in Ontario is 4.15 metres. You must also remember that road repairs, rough roads, ice and floods may cause difficulty where clearance is otherwise normally adequate.

You must follow instructions on signs posted where dangerous conditions exist and obey regulations that ban trucks on certain highways, at certain times or on certain days.

Turns and steering

Turning a large vehicle requires more care and knowledge than turning a

Diagram 2-7

Diagram 2-8

passenger car. Besides observing the general turn rules outlined in the *Official MTO Driver's Handbook*, you must keep other factors in mind.

For example, during a given turn of the steering wheel, the rear wheels follow a shorter path than those up front. Allow this on all turns so that your vehicle doesn't strike another vehicle or stationary object.

Steering (forward) and off-track

The rear wheels of the vehicle do not pivot and therefore will not follow the same path as the front wheels. The greater the distance (wheel base) between the front wheels and the rear wheels of the vehicle, the greater the amount of "off-track." The off-track path has a shorter radius than the path of the front wheels.

On the open highway, you must lead your turning arc of the front wheels according to the sharpness of the curve and the amount of off-track of your vehicle (Diagrams 2-7 and 2-8). A curve to the right requires keeping the front wheels close to the left side of the lane to prevent dropping the rear wheels off the pavement. A curve to the left requires keeping the front wheels close to the right edge of the pavement to prevent the rear wheels from crossing into the other traffic lane.

A combination vehicle such as a semi-trailer unit has an off-track of the rear wheels of the tractor unit, and a greater off-track again of the rear wheels of a semi.

The combination unit of a truck-tractor and semi-trailer has different turning characteristics. These units have a turning radius and off-track pattern within each unit, but the amount of off-track depends upon the length of the combination and the wheel base of the units.

Whenever possible, turns must be made from the proper lanes. When it becomes necessary for you to direct your vehicle over lane lines or centre lines to negotiate sharp turns, it is your responsibility to be sure that the movement can be made safely, without interfering with other traffic.

Right turns

Right turns at intersections with vehicles that have a lot of off-track require you to lead the turning arc according to the amount of off-track, otherwise you run the risk of running the rear wheels of the unit over curbs and sidewalks.

Remember that you may need to proceed well into the intersection before beginning the turn. Generally, it is better to use more space from the road you are leaving than from

Diagram 2-9

the road you are entering. Move as close to the left side of the your lane as possible and then make the turn, using the space you need to complete the turn from the road you are entering. However, depending on the type of vehicle you are driving and the width of the road's lanes, you may have to cross the centre line or travel into the second traffic lane of the street entered.

If you are driving a tractor-trailer on a narrow street, for example, you will have to use some, or all, of the left lane in order to get your vehicle around the corner without the rear wheels of your unit going up on the curb. Use extreme caution and ensure the movement can be made safely. When it is necessary to "block" off another traffic lane, make sure that smaller vehicles, motorcycles or cyclists are not attempting to move up along the right side of your vehicle. The critical point is reached when the tractor is at the sharpest point of the turn in relation to the trailer, because vision through your right rear view mirror is limited.

Left turns

You must be aware of and allow for any off-track when making a left turn. Unless you use your left outside mirror to monitor the trailer's path, the trailer might hit either a vehicle or a sign post on an island.

You must turn the vehicle in a wide arc before bringing it back to its proper position after a left turn, just right of the centre line; then, as you increase speed, you can move, when it is safe, to the right lane.

Backing

Planning your route in advance may eliminate the need for backing. If necessary, drive around the block if it will help you to avoid backing around a corner. Drive out into traffic rather than backing into traffic. Avoid entering the path of

Diagram 2-10

a reversing vehicle and do not stop or park behind a vehicle that may soon be reversed. As the driver, you are responsible for ensuring all precautions are taken when attempting to back into a driveway from the road.

- Prior to backing: Turn off phone/radio, open windows, activate four-way flashers and sound horn.
- Exit the vehicle and walk around to examine the area into which you must back. Look for overhead obstacles or wires, side clearances,

pedestrians or objects in your path of travel.
- Remember to use both rearview mirrors. Keep in mind the blind spot on the rear, as vision is limited.

Straight backing

The easiest and safest backing manoeuvre is straight backing. Whenever possible use this approach.

- Pull ahead and position the tractor and trailer in line with the direction you want it to take.

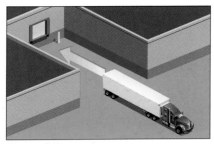

Diagram 2-11

- Ensure front and rear wheels are straight and centred.
- Watch both mirrors while backing slowly in a straight line.
- If the trailer drifts left or right, align the vehicle accordingly.

Alley dock (driver's side)

When performing an alley dock, backing from the driver's side is recommended.

- Position your vehicle so that the trailer is angled in the direction you want it to take.
- Turn steering wheel hard to the right while backing slowly.
- Look out driver's window to monitor trailer while checking mirrors.
- If the turn is too early or sharp, turn wheels slightly to the left accordingly. If the turn is too late or wide, adjust wheels by turning it to the right.

Offset backing (driver's side)

There are two types of offset backing: driver side where you offset back to the left; and passenger side where you offset back to the right.

- Drive straight forward until the vehicle is in a straight line.
- Turn the wheel all the way to the left angling the trailer toward the destination.
- Back up while watching the right mirror until the outside edge of the tractor tires lines up with the middle of the landing gear.
- Stop and turn the wheel to the right as far as possible.
- Back up until the tractor is straight and in line with the trailer.
- Straighten the wheels. Look out both mirrors while slowly backing toward the destination.

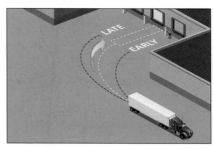

Diagram 2-12

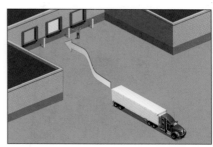

Diagram 2-13

Guide

A responsible guide can help you by watching the area into which you are backing and by keeping an eye on your blind-spot zone. The guide should stand in a position to see you and the area to the rear of your vehicle clearly. They should also be prepared to warn you if pedestrians or vehicles move into your path as you back. This can help you make an easy and safe approach to the dock. Remember that back-up alarm devices do not relieve the driver's responsibility when reversing.

Chapter 2-Summary

By the end of this chapter you should know:

- Where to position your vehicle when stopping at stoplights and stop signs
- The importance of stopping at railway crossings and how to position your vehicle to stop for them
- How and when to stop for school crossings and school buses
- How and when to stop for pedestrian crossovers
- The use of the transmission, differential lock and the braking system
- The importance of knowing your vehicle's height and width
- How to steer in forward, reverse and while turning
- The meaning of "off-track" and where to position your vehicle on the road
- How and when to back up; straight backing; how to perform an alley dock from the driver's side; and offset backing from the driver's side.

CHAPTER 3
SAFE AND RESPONSIBLE DRIVING

I. PRECAUTIONS

Observe the laws governing the operation of a motor vehicle scrupulously and make every effort to follow good driving practice and safety rules.

- Back a truck with the utmost care and caution. Use all rearview mirrors, turn and look back and, if possible, have someone give you directions. Back slowly and cautiously and watch traffic conditions around the vehicle at all times.
- Bad weather requires changing your driving procedures. Exercise exceptional care in such conditions.

- Adjust your speed to meet road, weather and traffic conditions.
- Never load a truck beyond its licensed capacity.
- Avoid situations that call for quick stops.
- Never allow an unauthorized person to occupy the driver's seat, operate the truck or any of its controls.

II. DRIVER CONDUCT

Today's truck drivers are among the most visible citizens on the highways, and the motoring public tends to criticize some of their driving practices. So it's up to responsible truck drivers to influence the public's opinion. Be a defensive driver, anticipate what other drivers might do and compensate for them.

1. **Obstructing traffic:** Slowing down on hills is often unavoidable, but good drivers can reduce the delay to faster vehicles by being aware of the following traffic and staying to the right, allowing following traffic to pass. It is a good safety practice to activate your hazard lights when unable to keep to traffic speed. Never use your left-turn signals to tell following motorists it is safe to pass. It is against the law and tends to confuse other drivers, who may think you are signaling a left turn or lane change.

2. **Improper passing:** Some truck drivers switch on their turn signals and immediately pull out into traffic when the traffic stream is too close and dense. Another complaint is the practice of pulling out to pass another large vehicle on a multiple-lane highway when the difference in speed is so small that the manoeuvre obstructs following traffic for an unreasonable period of time. Avoid these errors.

3. **Bluffing:** Drivers who use the large size of their vehicles to intimidate others and force their way through traffic may create serious hazards.

4. **Following:** When a number of trucks pull onto a highway after a stop, drivers should do so at intervals that will allow them to leave sufficient space. Commercial motor vehicles must maintain a minimum distance of at least 60 metres (200 ft.) between themselves and other vehicles when on a highway at a speed exceeding 60 km/h (40 mph), except when overtaking and passing another motor vehicle.

5. **Speed limiter:** Requirements will apply to vehicles that were manufactured in 1995 or newer with a manufacturer's gross vehicle weight rating (MGVWR) of 11,794 kilograms (26,000 lbs.) or more. Only commercial motor vehicles with an electronically controlled engine are subject to these regulatory requirements.

The speed-limiting system of these commercial motor vehicles shall be properly set to no more than 105 km/h (65 mph).

Buses, mobile cranes, motor homes, ambulances, cardiac-arrest emergency vehicles and fire apparatuses will be exempt from the regulation.

III. SHARING THE ROAD
Sharing the road with smaller vehicles

Be aware that most drivers of smaller vehicles do not understand what it is like to drive a large vehicle such as a tractor-trailer. Many do not realize that a tractor-trailer needs twice as much stopping distance as the average car, and takes much longer to get up to normal driving speed. Many drivers also feel nervous when a large vehicle comes up behind or beside them, and this may cause them to make sudden or unexpected moves.

Here are some tips for sharing the road with smaller vehicles:

1. **Following:** It is very dangerous to follow too closely behind another vehicle. If something unexpected occurs, you will not have enough room to stop safely. Also, be aware that a large vehicle looming up closely behind may intimidate drivers of small vehicles.

2. **Being passed:** Be courteous when smaller, faster vehicles are trying to pass you. Slow down enough to allow the vehicle to fit in quickly and safely in front of you.

3. **Signalling:** Signal your intentions clearly before turning, slowing or stopping so that other drivers will have adequate time to react appropriately.

4. **Turning:** Many drivers of smaller vehicles do not understand how much room large vehicles need in order to make a turn. Drivers of smaller vehicles will often drive up into the large vehicle's turning space, not realizing until too late that the large vehicle needs that space to complete the turn. To safely complete a turn, you should proceed slowly and observe the rear of the vehicle. Always check to make sure a vehicle has not moved up into your turning space before completing your turn.

Diagram 3-1

Diagram 3-2

Sharing the road with motorcycles, limited-speed motorcycles or mopeds

Motorcycles, limited-speed motor-cycles and mopeds are harder to see because of their size. Drivers of these vehicles may make sudden moves because of uneven road surfaces or poor weather conditions. Because they are less protected, they are more likely to be injured in a collision.

Motorcycles and mopeds that cannot keep up with traffic should drive as close as possible to the right edge of the road; however, remember that these vehicles have the right to use the whole lane.

Since many motorcycle turn signals do not automatically shut off, be careful when turning left in front of an oncoming motorcycle with its turn signal on. Make sure the motorcyclist is actually turning; he or she may have just forgotten to switch off the turn signal.

Sharing the road with cyclists

Bicycles and mopeds travelling at a lower speed than other traffic are expected to ride about one metre from the curb or parked cars, or as close as practical to the right-hand edge of the road when there is no curb. However, they can use any part of the lane if necessary for safety, such as to:

- Avoid obstacles such as puddles, ice, sand, debris, rutted or grooved pavement, potholes and sewer grates
- Cross railway or streetcar tracks at a 90° angle
- Discourage passing where the lane is too narrow to be shared safely

Cyclists are not required to ride close to the right edge of the road when they are travelling at or faster than the normal speed of traffic at that time and place, or when they are turning left, or getting in position to turn left. (Cyclists are permitted to make a left turn from a left-turn lane, where one is available.)

When passing a cyclist, as a best practice, allow at least one metre between your vehicle and the cyclist. Whenever possible, you should change lanes to pass.

Do not follow too closely behind cyclists. They do not have brake lights to warn you when they are slowing or stopping.

Intersections – To avoid colli-sions with bicyclists at intersections, remember the following:

- When turning right, signal and check your mirrors and the blind spot to your right to make sure you do not cut off a cyclist.
- When turning left, you must stop and wait for oncoming bicycles to pass before turning.
- When driving through an intersec-tion, be careful to scan for cyclists waiting to turn left.

Do not sound your horn unnecessarily when you are overtaking a cyclist. It may frighten them and cause them to lose control. If you feel that you must use your horn, tap it quickly and lightly while you are still some distance away from the cyclist.

Bike lanes are reserved for cyclists. They are typically marked by a solid white line. Sometimes you will need to enter or cross a bike lane to turn right at a corner or driveway. Take extra care when you do this. Enter the bike lane only after ensuring that you can do so safely, and then make the turn.

Watch for cyclists' hand signals. A cyclist may indicate a right-hand turn by extending their right arm.

Try to make eye contact when possible with cyclists.

Bike boxes help prevent collisions between motorists and bicycles at intersections. It is typically a painted box on the road with a white

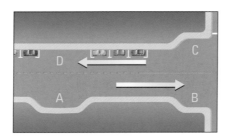

Diagram 3-3

A   Mid-block indented bays
B   An indentation before an intersection
C   An indentation after an intersection
D   Bus stops between legally parked cars

bicycle symbol inside. Bicycle lanes approaching and leaving the box may also be painted. As a driver, you must stop for a traffic signal behind the bike box. Do not stop in the box.

Children riding bicycles on the street may lack the necessary training and skills for safe cycling. They may not be aware of all the dangers or the rules of the road. Watch for children

on oversized bicycles as they may not have the ability to control it.

When parked on the side of the roadway, look behind you and check your mirrors and blind spots for a passing cyclist before opening a door.

Sharing the road with municipal buses

Many roadways have special indented stopping areas for municipal buses, called bus bays, where passengers can get on and off. There are three types of bus bays:

- Mid-block indented bays
- Indentations immediately before and after intersections
- Bus-stop areas between two designated parking areas

When a bus in a bus bay begins flashing its left-turn signals, indicating that it is ready to leave the bus bay, and you are approaching in the lane adjacent to the bus bay, you must allow the bus to re-enter traffic.

Sharing the road with farm machinery

Farm machinery moves quite slowly compared to other road users. Most tractors and combines have a maximum speed of 40 km/h, but travel at less than 40 km/h when towing implements or wagons. Farm machinery is often oversized, wide or long or both, making it difficult for the driver to see vehicles coming up from behind. Farmers often turn directly into fields rather than roads or lanes, or move from lane to lane. Remember that it is common for farmers to be on the roads after dark during peak planting and harvesting seasons. Farm machinery on the road must display an orange and red slow-moving vehicle sign on the rear of the vehicle. The sign warns other drivers that the vehicle is travelling at 40 km/h or less. If you see one of these signs, slow down and be cautious. Stay well back and do not pass until it is safe to do so. (See the slow-moving vehicle sign on page 87.)

Sharing the road with pedestrians

Pay special attention to pedestrians, whether they are crossing roads in traffic, walking or jogging alongside roads, or using crosswalks or crossovers (generally known as crossings). Drivers should be aware of pedestrians who often will jaywalk not just cross at intersections. **Note** that a ball bouncing into the roadway may be followed by a child or animal. Watch for children. Drive slowly and cautiously through school zones, residential areas and any other area where children may be walking or playing. You never know when a child might dart out from between parked cars or try to cross a street without checking for oncoming traffic. Be very cautious at twilight when children may still be playing outside, but are very difficult to see. Watch out for Community Safety Zone signs as they indicate areas where the community has identified that there is a special risk to pedestrians.

Diagram 3-4

Seniors or pedestrains with disabilities need extra caution and courtesy from drivers, as they may be slow in crossing the road. Be alert for pedestrians with visual or hearing disabilities, those who use wheelchairs or walk slowly due to some other physical disabilities, and give them appropriate consideration. Pedestrians who are blind or with a visual disability may use a white cane or guide dog to help them travel safely along sidewalks and across intersections. Caution signs are posted in some areas where there is a special need for drivers to be alert.

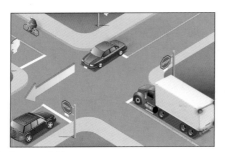

Diagram 3-5

Diagram 3-6

Diagram 3-7

Persons operating mobility devices (motorized wheelchair and medical scooters) are treated the same way as pedestrians. Usually these people will travel along a sidewalk, but if there is no sidewalk available, they should travel, like pedestrians, along the left shoulder of the roadway facing oncoming traffic.

Some streetcar stops have a special safety island or zone for passengers getting on and off. Pass these safety islands and zones at a reasonable speed. Always be ready in case pedestrians make sudden or unexpected moves.

Yielding the right-of-way

There are times when you must yield the right-of-way. This means you must let another person go first. Here are some rules about when you must yield the right-of-way:

- At an intersection without signs or lights, you must yield the right-of-way to any vehicle approaching from the right (Diagram 3-4).
- At an intersection with stop signs at all corners, you must yield the right-of-way to the first vehicle to come to a complete stop. If two vehicles stop at the same time, the vehicle on the left must yield to the

vehicle on the right (Diagram 3-5).
- At any intersection where you want to turn left or right, you must yield the right-of-way. If you are turning left, you must wait for approaching traffic to pass or turn and for pedestrians in your path to cross. If you are turning right, you must wait for pedestrians to cross (Diagram 3-6).
- A yield sign means you must slow down or stop if necessary and yield the right-of-way to traffic in the intersection or on the intersecting road.

Diagram 3-8

- When entering a road from a private road or driveway, you must yield to vehicles on the road and pedestrians on the sidewalk (Diagram 3-7).
- You must yield the right-of-way and wait for pedestrians to completely cross the road at specially marked pedestrian crossings or crossovers (Diagram 3-8) as well as school crossings with crossing guards.

Remember: Signalling does not give you the right-of-way. You must make sure the way is clear.

Driving in roundabouts

Allow extra room alongside large vehicles (trucks and buses). They may have to swing wide on the approach or within the roundabout. Give them plenty of room.

Pull over for emergency vehicles

If you are in a roundabout when an emergency vehicle approaches, continue to your intended exit and proceed beyond the traffic island before pulling over. If you have not entered the roundabout yet, pull over to the right if possible and wait until the emergency vehicle has passed.

Driving a large vehicle in a roundabout

A driver negotiating a roundabout in a large vehicle (such as a truck or bus) may need to use the full width of the roadway, including the central apron (a mountable portion of the centre island adjacent to the roadway) if provided. Prior to entering the roundabout, the vehicle may need to occupy both lanes. Give large vehicles plenty of room to manoeuvre.

Many roundabouts are also designed with a central apron, a raised section of pavement around the central island that acts as an extra lane for large vehicles. The back wheels of the oversize vehicle can ride up on the central apron so the truck can easily complete the turn, while the raised portion of concrete discourages use by smaller vehicles.

Diagram 3-9

10 WAYS YOU CAN HELP MAKE ONTARIO'S ROADS THE SAFEST IN NORTH AMERICA

1. Don't drink and drive. Don't drive when you're taking medication that will affect your driving.

2. Always wear your seat belt.

3. Obey the speed limits. Slow down when road and weather conditions are poor.

4. Don't take risks: don't cut people off in traffic, make sudden lane changes or run yellow lights.

5. Don't drive when you're tired, upset or sick.

6. If you're in doubt, let the other driver go first — yield the right-of-way.

7. Keep a safe distance between your vehicle and the one ahead.

8. Avoid distractions such as loud music and cell phones.

9. Check your mirrors frequently; always check your blind spot before you change lanes.

10. Check traffic in all directions before going into an intersection.

IV. DRIVING AT NIGHT AND IN BAD WEATHER

At night and in weather conditions such as rain, snow or fog, you cannot see as far ahead, even with headlights. Slow down when driving at night, especially on unlit roads, and whenever weather conditions reduce your visibility.

Overdriving your headlights

You are overdriving your headlights when your stopping distance is farther than you can see with your headlights. This is a dangerous thing to do because you may not give yourself enough room to make a safe stop. Reflective road signs can mislead you as well, making you believe you can see farther than you really can. This may cause you to overdrive your headlights if you are not careful.

Glare

Glare is dazzling light that makes it hard for you to see and be aware of what others around you are doing.

It can be a problem on both sunny and overcast days, depending on the angle of the sun's rays and your surroundings. Glare can also be a problem at night when you face bright headlights or see them reflected in your mirrors.

When meeting oncoming vehicles with bright headlights at night, look up and beyond and slightly to the right of the oncoming lights. In daytime glare, use your sun visor or use a pair of good quality sunglasses. When you enter a tunnel on a bright day, slow down to let your eyes adjust to the reduced light. Remove your sunglasses and turn on your headlights.

Cut down glare at night by following the rules of the road for vehicle lights. Use your low-beam headlights within 150 metres (500 ft.) of an oncoming vehicle or when following a vehicle within 60 metres (200 ft.). On country roads, switch to low beams when you come to a curve or hilltop so you can see oncoming headlights and won't blind oncoming drivers. If you can't see any headlights, switch back to high beams.

Fog

Fog is a thin layer of cloud resting on the ground. Fog can reduce visibility for drivers, resulting in difficult driving conditions.

The best thing to do is to avoid driving in fog. Check weather forecasts and, if there is a fog warning, delay your trip until it clears. If that is not possible or you get caught driving in fog, there are a number of safe driving tips you should follow. If visibility is decreasing rapidly, move off the road and into a safe parking area to wait for the fog to lift.

TIPS FOR DRIVING SAFELY IN FOG

Before you drive—and during your trip—check weather forecasts. If there is a fog warning, delay your trip until it clears. It could save your life. If you are caught driving in fog, follow these safe driving tips:

DO:
* Slow down gradually and drive at a speed that suits the conditions.
* Make sure the full lighting system of your vehicle is turned on.
* Use your low-beam headlights. High beams reflect off the moisture droplets in the fog, making it harder to see.
* If you have fog lights on your vehicle, use them, in addition to your low beams.
* Be patient. Avoid passing, changing lanes and crossing traffic.

* Use pavement markings to help guide you. Use the right edge of the road as a guide, rather than the centre line.
* Increase your following distance. You will need extra distance to brake safely.
* Look and listen for any hazards that may be ahead.
* Reduce the distractions in your vehicle. For example, turn off your cell phone. Your full attention is required.
* Watch for any electronically operated warning signs.
* Keep looking as far ahead as possible.
* Keep your windows and mirrors clean. Use your defroster and wipers to maximize your vision.
* If the fog is too dense to continue, pull completely off the road and try to position your vehicle in a safe parking area. Turn on your emergency flashers, in addition to keeping your low-beam headlights on.

DON'T:
* Don't stop on the travelled portion of the road. You could become the first link in a chain-reaction collision.
* Don't speed up suddenly, even if the fog seems to be clearing. You could find yourself suddenly back in fog.
* Don't speed up to pass a vehicle moving slowly or to get away from a vehicle that is following too closely.

REMEMBER:
* Watch your speed. You may be going faster than you think. If so, reduce speed gradually.
* Leave a safe braking distance between you and the vehicle ahead.
* Remain calm and patient. Don't pass other vehicles or speed up suddenly.
* Don't stop on the road. If visibility is decreasing rapidly, pull off the road into a safe parking area and wait for the fog to lift.
* Use your low-beam lights.

Rain

Rain makes road surfaces slippery, especially as the first drops fall. With more rain, tires make less contact with the road. If there is too much water or if you are going too fast, your tires may ride on top of the water, like water skis. This is called hydroplaning. When this happens, control becomes very difficult. Make sure you have good tires with deep tread, and slow down when the road is wet.

Rain also reduces visibility. Drive slowly enough to be able to stop within the distance you can see. Make sure your windshield wipers are in good condition. If your wiper blades do not clean the windshield without streaking, replace them.

In rain, try to drive on clear sections of road. Look ahead and plan your movements. Smooth steering, braking and accelerating will reduce the chance of skids. Leave more space between you and the vehicle ahead in case you have to stop. This will also help you to avoid spray from the vehicle ahead that can make it even harder to see.

Avoid driving in puddles. A puddle can hide a large pothole that could damage your vehicle or its suspension, or flatten a tire. The spray of water could obstruct the vision of adjacent motorists and result in a collision, cause harm to nearby pedestrians or drown your engine, causing it to stall. Water can also make your brakes less effective.

Flooded roads

Avoid driving on flooded roads–water may prevent your brakes from working. If you must drive through a flooded stretch of road, test your brakes afterwards to dry them out.

Test your brakes when it is safe to do so by stopping quickly and firmly at 50 km/h. Make sure the vehicle stops in a straight line, without pulling to one side. The brake pedal should feel firm and secure, not spongy–that's a sign of trouble.

If you still feel a pulling to one side or a spongy brake pedal even after the brakes are dry, you should take the vehicle in for repair immediately.

Skids

A skid may happen when one or more tires lose their grip with the road's surface. Skids most often happen on a slippery surface, such as a road that is wet, icy or covered with snow, gravel or some other loose material. Most skids result from driving too fast for road conditions. Hard braking and overly aggressive turning or accelerating can cause your vehicle to skid and possibly go out of control.

To avoid a skid on a slippery road, drive at a reduced speed and operate the vehicle's controls in a smooth and constrained manner. Increasing tire forces, such as by braking or accelerating while steering may push tires even closer to a skid condition. It's essential that the vehicle's speed be maintained at a safe level and that turns be made gently.

If your vehicle begins to skid, try not to panic – it is possible to maintain control of your vehicle, even in a skid. Ease off on the accelerator or brake and, on a very slippery surface, slip the transmission into neutral if you can. Continue to steer in the direction you wish to go. Be careful not to oversteer. Once you regain control you can brake as needed, but very gently and smoothly.

Anti-lock Brakes–If your vehicle is equipped with anti-lock brakes, practise emergency braking to understand how your vehicle will react. It is a good idea to practise doing this under controlled conditions with a qualified driving instructor.

Anti-lock braking systems (ABS) are designed to sense the speed of the wheels on a vehicle during braking. An abnormal drop in wheel speed, which indicates potential wheel lock, causes the brake force to be reduced to that wheel. This is how the anti-lock braking system prevents tire skid and the accompanying loss of steering control. This improves vehicle safety during heavy brake use or when braking with poor traction.

Although ABS helps to prevent wheel lock, you should not expect the stopping distance for your vehicle to be shortened.

Drivers unfamiliar with ABS may be surprised by the pulsations that they may feel in the brake pedal when they brake hard. Make sure you know what to expect so you will not be distracted by the pulsation or tempted to release the pedal during emergency braking manoeuvres.

Threshold Braking–Threshold braking should bring you to a reasonably quick, controlled stop in your own lane, even in slippery conditions. This technique is generally practised in a vehicle that is not equipped with ABS. Brake as hard as you can until a wheel begins to lock up, then release pressure on the pedal slightly to release the wheel. Press down on the brake pedal, applying as much braking force as possible without inducing a skid. If you feel any of the wheels begin to lock up, release the brake pressure slightly and re-apply. Don't pump the brakes. Continue braking this way until you have slowed the vehicle to the desired speed.

Vehicles equipped with ABS should provide controlled braking, on slippery surfaces automatically. Press the brake pedal hard and allow the system to control wheel lock up.

TIPS FOR DRIVING IN BLOWING SNOW AND WHITEOUT CONDITIONS

Before you drive—and during your trip—check weather forecasts and road reports. If there is a weather warning, or reports of poor visibility and driving conditions, delay your trip until conditions improve, if possible. If you get caught driving in blowing snow or a whiteout, follow these safe driving tips:

DO:
- Slow down gradually and drive at a speed that suits the conditions.
- Make sure the full lighting system of your vehicle is turned on.
- Use your low-beam headlights. High beams reflect off the ice particles in the snow, making it harder to see.
- If you have fog lights on your vehicle, use them, in addition to your low beams.
- Be patient. Avoid passing, changing lanes and crossing traffic.
- Increase your following distance. You will need extra space to brake safely.
- Stay alert. Keep looking as far ahead as possible.
- Reduce the distractions in your vehicle. Your full attention is required. Keep your windows and mirrors clean. Use defroster and wipers to maximize your vision.
- Try to get off the road when visibility is near zero. Pull into a safe parking area if possible.

DON'T:
- Don't stop on the travelled portion of the road. You could become the first link in a chain-reaction collision.
- Don't attempt to pass a vehicle moving slowly or speed up to get away from a vehicle that is following too closely.

REMEMBER:
- Watch your speed. You may be going faster than you think. If so, reduce speed gradually.
- Leave a safe braking distance between you and the vehicle ahead.
- Stay alert, remain calm and be patient.
- If visibility is decreasing rapidly, do not stop on the road. Look for an opportunity to pull off the road into a safe parking area and wait for conditions to improve.
- If you become stuck or stranded in severe weather, stay with your vehicle for warmth and safety until help arrives. Open a window slightly for ventilation. Run your motor sparingly. Use your emergency flashers.
- Be prepared and carry a winter-driving survival kit that includes items such as warm clothing, non-perishable energy foods, flashlight, shovel and blanket.
- Look ahead and watch for clues that indicate you need to slow down and anticipate slippery road conditions.

Snow

Snow may be hard-packed, slippery as ice, rutted, full of hard tracks and gullies, or smooth and soft. Look ahead and anticipate what you must do based on the snow conditions. Slow down on rutted snowy roads. Avoid sudden steering, braking or accelerating that could cause a skid.

Whiteouts

Blowing snow may create whiteouts where snow completely blocks your view of the road. When blowing snow is forecast, drive only if necessary and with extreme caution.

Ice

As temperatures drop below freezing, wet roads become icy. Sections of road in shaded areas or on bridges and overpasses freeze first. It is important to look ahead, slow down and anticipate ice.

If the road ahead looks like black and shiny asphalt, be suspicious. It may be covered with a thin layer of ice known as black ice. Generally, asphalt in the winter should look gray-white in colour. If you think there may be black ice ahead, slow down and be careful.

Snow plows

Snow-removal vehicles on public roadways are equipped with flashing blue lights that can be seen from 150 metres.

Flashing blue lights warn you of wide and slow-moving vehicles. Some snow plows have a wing that extends as far as three metres to the right of the vehicle. On freeways, several snow plows may be staggered across the road, clearing all lanes at the same time by passing a ridge of snow from plow to plow. Do not try to pass between them. This is extremely dangerous because there is not enough room to pass safely, and the ridge of wet snow can throw your vehicle out of control.

V. DEALING WITH PARTICULAR SITUATIONS

Drowsy driving

Drowsiness has been identified as a causal factor in a growing number of collisions resulting in injury and fatality. Tired drivers can be as impaired as drunk drivers. They have a slower reaction time and are less alert.

Studies have shown that collisions involving drowsiness tend to occur during late night/early morning hours (between 2 a.m. and 6 a.m.) or late afternoon (between 2 p.m. and 4 p.m.) Studies also indicate that shift workers, people with undiagnosed or untreated sleep disorders and commercial vehicle operators are at greater risk for such collisions.

Always avoid driving when you are feeling drowsy. Scientific research confirms that you can fall asleep without actually being aware of it. Here are eight important warning signs that your drowsiness is serious enough to place you at risk:

- You have difficulty keeping your eyes open.
- Your head keeps tilting forward despite your efforts to keep your eyes on the road.
- Your mind keeps wandering and you can't seem to concentrate.
- You yawn frequently.
- You can't remember details about the last few kilometres you have travelled.
- You are missing traffic lights and signals.
- Your vehicle drifts into the next lane and you have to jerk it back into your lane.
- You have drifted off the road and narrowly avoided a crash.

If you have one of these symptoms, you may be in danger of falling asleep. Pull off the road and park your vehicle in a safe, secure place. Use well-lit rest stops or truck stops on busy roads. Lock your doors, roll up your windows and take a nap.

Stimulants are never a substitute for sleep. Drinks containing caffeine can help you feel more alert, but if you are sleep deprived, the effects wear off quickly. The same is true of turning up the volume of your radio or CD player and opening the window. You cannot trick your body into staying awake; you need to sleep. Remember, the only safe driver is a well-rested, alert driver.

Aggressive driving and road rage

Aggressive-driving behaviours, such as tailgating, speeding, failing to yield the right-of-way and cutting in front of someone too closely, may cause other drivers to become frustrated and angry, and lead to a road-rage conflict between drivers. An angry driver may attempt dangerous retaliatory action. Avoid becoming angry on the road by following these tips:

- Know the warning signs of stress, and combat them by getting fresh air, breathing deeply and slowly, and listening to relaxing music.

- Make a conscious decision not to take your problems with you when driving.
- If you are on a long trip, take a break from driving every few hours.
- Don't compete with another driver, or retaliate for what you believe to be inconsiderate behaviour.
- If someone else's driving annoys you, don't try to "educate" the person. Leave traffic enforcement to the police.
- Don't take other drivers' mistakes or behaviours personally.
- Avoid honking your horn at other drivers, unless absolutely necessary. A light tap on the horn is usually sufficient.

Remember that, if you drive responsibly and courteously, you are less likely to spark a road-rage situation.

- Plan your route in advance. Some of the most erratic and inconsiderate driving occurs when a driver is lost.
- Drive in a courteous and considerate manner.
- Yield the right-of-way when it is courteous to do so.
- Be polite and let other drivers in front of you when they are signalling that they would like to do so.
- If you make a mistake while driving, indicate that you are sorry. An apology can greatly reduce the risk of conflict.
- Don't return aggression. Avoid eye contact and do not gesture back. Keep away from erratic drivers.

If you are in a situation in which you feel threatened by another driver, do the following:
- Stay in your vehicle and lock the doors.
- If you have a cell phone, call police.

- Use your horn and signals to attract attention.
- If you believe you are being followed, do not drive home. Drive to a police station or a busy public place.

Workers on the road

Be extra careful when driving through construction zones and areas where people are working on or near the road.

When approaching a construction zone, proceed with caution and obey all warning signs, people and/or devices that are directing traffic through the area. Often, lower speed limits are posted to increase worker safety and reflect increased road hazards, such as construction vehicles in the area, uneven or gravel surfaces, narrowed lanes and so on. In a construction zone, drive carefully and adjust your driving to suit the conditions. Do not change lanes, be ready for sudden stops and watch for workers and related construction vehicles and equipment on the road.

Other types of workers and vehicles may also be present on the road and pose a hazard, such as roadside assistance and disabled vehicles, surveyors, road-maintenance or utility workers. Always, slow down and pass with caution to prevent a collision. If safe to do so, move over a lane to increase the space between your vehicle and the hazard.

Animals on the road

Crashes involving animals (mainly moose and deer) are a growing problem. You may encounter domestic, farm or wild animals on the road anywhere in Ontario. The number of animals hit by vehicles increased from 7,388 in 1994 to 13,729 in 2003, an 86-percent increase over a 10-year period.

Many areas of the province have animal-crossing signs that warn drivers of the danger of large animals (such as moose, deer or cattle) crossing the road. Be cautious when you see these signs, especially during dusk-to-dawn hours when wild animals are most active.

To reduce your chances of hitting an animal:
- Reduce speed in darkness, rain and fog. These conditions can impair your ability to see an animal on or near the road.
- Travel at a safe speed and stay alert. Driver inattention and speed are common factors in animal/vehicle crashes.
- Scan the road ahead from shoulder to shoulder. If you see an animal on or near the road, slow down and pass carefully, as it may suddenly bolt in front of you.
- Watch for shining eyes at the roadside. If you do see shining eyes, slow down and be ready to stop.
- Keep your windshield clean and headlights properly adjusted.
- Use high beams whenever possible and safe to do so, and scan both sides of the road ahead.

If you see an animal:
- Slow down and sound your horn.
- Be alert for other animals that may be with the one you've seen.
- Don't try to drive around the animal. Animal movements are unpredictable.
- If you wish to watch an animal, find a safe place to pull completely off the road and park first. Do not park on the shoulder of the road, as other drivers may be distracted by the animal and hit your vehicle.
- Stay in your vehicle; getting out increases your chance of being hit by another vehicle.
- If you hit a deer or moose, report it to the local police service or the Ministry of Natural Resources. Do not try to move an injured animal.

Distracted driving

Driving while using non-hands-free cellular phones and viewing display screens unrelated to driving is prohibited, and drivers will face fines and other penalties. In addition, drivers can be charged with careless driving or even dangerous driving (a criminal offence) if they do not pay full attention to the driving task.

Note: Commercial drivers have a permanent exemption for the use of a two-way radio, provided the microphone is securely mounted to the vehicle within easy reach of the driver. This allows the driver to press and hold the microphone button to talk and release to listen.

Even if your vehicle has driver-assistance features, you can be charged with distracted, careless or dangerous driving. You are still expected to be in care and control of your vehicle, which means that you must be constantly monitoring your environment and able to take over immediate control of the vehicle.

TIPS TO REDUCE DRIVER DISTRACTIONS

- Attend to personal grooming and plan your route before you leave.
- Identify and preset your vehicle's climate control and audio settings.
- Make it a habit to pull over and park to use your cell phone or have a passenger take the call or let it go to voice mail.
- Put reading material away if you are tempted to read.
- Do not engage in emotional or complex conversations. Stress can affect your driving performance.
- When you are hungry or thirsty, take a break from driving.

Remember to focus on your driving at all times. A split-second distraction behind the wheel can result in injury or even death.

Reacting to an approaching emergency vehicle

When you see red or red **and** blue flashing lights or hear the bells or sirens of an emergency vehicle approaching from either direction, you must immediately slow down, move as far to the right side of the roadway as you can and stop.

Stay alert. When you see an approaching emergency vehicle with its lights or siren on, prepare to clear the way.

- React quickly but calmly. Don't slam on the brakes or pull over suddenly. Use your signals to alert other drivers you intend to pull over.
- Check your rearview mirrors. Look in front and on both sides of your vehicle. Allow other vehicles to also pull over. Pull to the right and gradually come to a stop.
- Wait for the emergency vehicle to pass, and watch for other emergency vehicles that may be responding to the same call.

Emergency vehicles

Emergency vehicles (police, fire, ambulance and public utility emergency vehicles) are easily identified when responding to an emergency through their use of flashing red lights (police may also use red and blue flashing lights), a siren or bell, or alternating flashes of white light from their headlamp high beams. Also, be aware that police, fire and ambulance services use many different types of vehicles, including bicycles, snowmobiles, all-terrain vehicles, motorcycles, buses and trucks.

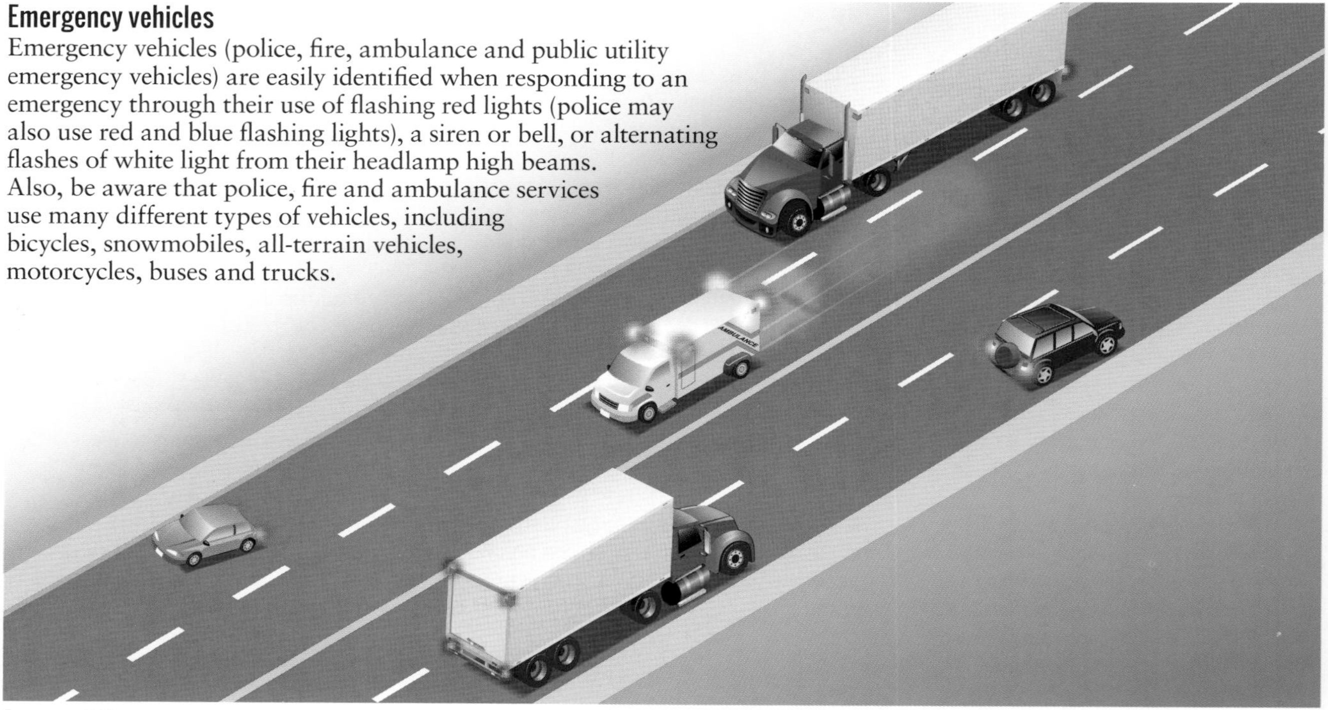

Diagram 3-10

Reacting to a stopped emergency vehicle or tow truck

When you see an emergency vehicle stopped with its red, or red and blue, flashing lights or a stopped tow truck with its amber lights flashing in a lane or on the shoulder in your direction of travel, you must slow down and pass with caution. If the road has two or more lanes, you must move over into another lane to allow one lane clearance between your vehicle and the emergency vehicle, if it can be done safely.
(Diagram 3-11)

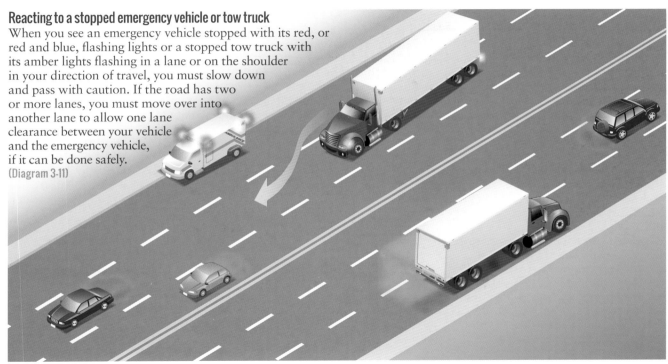

Diagram 3-11

Check to make sure the way is clear, and signal before merging back into traffic.

- Don't drive on or block the shoulder on freeways. Emergency vehicles will use the shoulder of the road if all lanes are blocked.

Never follow or try to outrun an emergency vehicle. It is illegal to follow within 150 metres of a fire vehicle or ambulance responding to a call in any lane going in the same direction. Failing to pull over and stop for an approaching emergency vehicle can result in a conviction and a fine.

Note: Some fire fighters and volunteer medical responders may display a flashing green light when using their own vehicles to respond to a fire or medical emergency. Please yield the right-of-way to help them reach the emergency quickly and safely.

Take lights and sirens seriously. Clear the way! Pull to the right and stop. It's the law.

Failing to follow these rules can result in a conviction, demerit points on your driving record, a driver's licence suspension of up to two years and a fine of $400 to $2,000 for a first offence and $1,000 to $4,000 for a "subsequent" offence. A "subsequent" offence is when you are convicted again within five years. The court can order you to spend up to six months in jail, or you may have to pay a fine, or both.

VI. DEALING WITH EMERGENCIES

Emergency warning devices and procedures

Every commercial motor vehicle on a provincial highway from one-half hour before sunset to one-half hour after sunrise must have a sufficient number of the following emergency warning devices:

- Flares, lamps or lanterns capable of continually producing two warning lights, each visible from a distance of at least 150 metres (500 ft.) for at least eight hours or
- Portable reflectors

Whenever any commercial motor vehicle or trailer is disabled, stalled, broken down or in a collision, the driver should quickly and calmly take the necessary actions to safeguard the vehicle and other motorists.

If the vehicle can be moved, move it as far off the roadway as safely possible — this should not affect the police officer's investigation. This is especially important on busy or high-speed roads where it may be dangerous to leave vehicles in the driving lanes.

1. Turn on your vehicle's emergency flashers/hazard warning signals.
2. During times when visibility is limited, your vehicle's low-beam headlights must be turned on.
3. In a speed limit zone greater than 60 km/h, if you cannot move your commercial vehicle off the roadway, you are required to set out one type of emergency warning device approximately 30 metres (100 ft.) to both the front and rear of your vehicle during times when visibility is limited.
4. It is recommended to use emergency warning devices for all emergencies, whether they occur during the day or night, or on-road or off the road, to ensure everyone's safety.

Note: Times of limited visibility are from one-half hour before sunset to one-half hour after sunrise, and any other time of poor light conditions, such as fog, snow or rain, which prevents clear visibility of people or vehicles less than 150 metres away. Do not park or leave your vehicle on a roadway unless it is not practical to move it off the roadway, or unless there is a clear view on the roadway for at least 125 metres (400 ft.) in both directions. Whenever the view of your vehicle is blocked by a hill, curve or other obstruction within 150 metres (500 ft.), an additional warning signal should be placed to give ample warning to other highway users.

Fire precautions

Commercial vehicle drivers should know how to prevent fires and have a basic knowledge of fire-fighting techniques. It's also essential to know what types of extinguisher or retardants to use on different types of fires.

Class A: fires include burning wood, paper, textiles, tires, etc.

Class B: fires include grease, oil, gasoline, solvents, paints, etc.

Class C: fires are those occurring in live electrical equipment.

Class D: fires include burning metals such as magnesium, sodium, potassium etc. Only special compounds suitable to the combustible metal involved should be used to extinguish fires on these materials.

Use all extinguishers according to the manufacturer's instructions. Some of the common causes for truck fires are:

- Running with a soft tire
- Overheated brakes, either from misuse or maladjustment. Check hub temperatures every time tires are checked
- Leaking fuel system, pump, filter, tanks or lines
- Unequal distribution of load, causing trailer to lean and rub on tires
- Careless smoking habits. Lighted cigarettes and cigars should always be butted in ashtrays, never thrown out windows. Never smoke while loading or unloading
- Carelessly placed flares, lamps or fuses used in an emergency
- Short circuits in the electrical system

There are various other reasons for fires, such as leaking exhaust systems or those that have been installed too close to fuel lines or wooden body parts. Occasionally, spontaneous combustion may occur in a van or trailer. Drivers must always know the nature of their cargoes, so necessary fire-control precautions can be taken.

When a fire occurs:

1. Stop the vehicle in a safe position away from buildings and other vehicles.
2. If it is a combination unit, uncouple the unit if possible.
3. If the fire occurs in or near a town, contact the fire department. Tell them what type of material is burning.
4. Based on the type of fire concerned, take all possible steps to extinguish it.
5. If the fire is thought to be due to a short-circuit, remove battery cables.
6. If the cargo is of an explosive nature, stop traffic and warn spectators to stay back.

In a collision where someone is injured or a fuel leak occurs

St. John Ambulance recommends that all drivers carry a well-stocked first-aid kit and know how to use it. Consider reading a book about first aid or sign up for a first-aid course. It could mean the difference between life and death in a collision.

Every driver involved in a collision must stay at the scene or return to it immediately and give all possible assistance. If you are not personally involved in a collision, you should stop to offer help if police or other help has not arrived.

In a collision with injuries, possible fuel leaks or serious vehicle damage, stay calm and follow these steps:

1. See the "Emergency warning devices and procedures" section in this book. Use caution if placing flares where fuel or flammable substances have leaked.

2. In response to these collisions, vehicles should not be moved, all engines should be turned off and approaching drivers should be warned.

3. Call for help or have someone else call. By law, you must report any collision to the police when there are injuries or damage to vehicles or other property exceeding $2,000.

4. Do not let anyone smoke, light a match or put flares near any vehicle in case of a fuel leak. If a vehicle is on fire, get the people out and make sure everyone is well out of the way. If there is no danger of fire or explosion, leave injured people where they are until trained medical help arrives.

5. If you are trained in first aid, treat injuries in the order of urgency, within the level of your training. For example, clear the person's airway to restore breathing, give rescue breathing or stop bleeding by applying pressure with a clean cloth.

6. If you are not trained in first aid, use common sense. For example, people in collisions often go into shock. Cover the person with a jacket or blanket to reduce the effects of shock.

7. Stay with injured people until help arrives.

8. Disabled vehicles on the road may be a danger to you and other drivers. Do what you can to make sure everyone involved in a collision is kept safe.

In a collision where no one is injured

Follow these steps in a collision where there are no injuries:

1. See "Emergency warning devices and procedures."
2. Call police (provincial or local, depending on where the collision takes place). By law, you must report any collision to the police-where there are injuries or damage to vehicles or property exceeding $2,000.
3. Give all possible help to police or anyone whose vehicle has been damaged. This includes giving police your name and address, the name and address of the registered owner of the vehicle, the vehicle plate and permit number, and the liability insurance card.
4. Get the names, addresses and phone numbers of all witnesses.
5. If damage is less than $2,000, you are still required by law to exchange information with anyone whose vehicle has been damaged. However, the collision does not have to be reported to the police.
6. Contact your insurance company as soon as possible if you intend to make a claim.

Chapter 3-Summary

By the end of this chapter you should know:

- The rules of etiquette for driving a large vehicle
- The importance of sharing the road with other road users, especially small vehicles, cyclists and pedestrians
- The concept of right-of-way and common situations where you must yield to other road users
- How to identify and manage situations where your visibility may be reduced
- How weather conditions such as rain, flooded roads, snow and ice may affect your vehicle and your ability to control it

- What to do if your vehicle skids or if you encounter heavy snow, whiteouts or black ice
- Recognizing and sharing the road with snow-removal vehicles
- Recognizing the signs of drowsiness and the importance of not driving when drowsy
- Recognizing the signs of aggressive driving both in yourself and other drivers; how to avoid road rage; and what to do if you find yourself in a situation involving aggressive driving or road rage
- How to manoeuvre your vehicle through construction zones
- What to do if you encounter animals on the road

- Things that may distract you when driving and how to minimize those distractions
- What to do when you encounter an emergency vehicle
- What to do in emergency situations when your vehicle stalls or breaks down
- How to prevent fires and basic fire-fighting techniques
- The steps to take if you are involved in a collision with or without injuries

CHAPTER 4
TRAFFIC SIGNS AND LIGHTS

Traffic laws include the traffic signs and lights, pedestrian signals and pavement markings that tell drivers and other road users what they must do in certain situations. This chapter shows you what many of those signs, lights and markings look like and explains what they mean to drivers.

I. SIGNS

Traffic signs give you important information about the law, warn you about dangerous conditions and help you find your way. Signs use different symbols, colours and shapes for easy identification.

Here are some of the many signs you will see on Ontario roads:

 A stop sign is eight-sided and has a red background and white letters. It means you must come to a complete stop. Stop at the stop line if it is marked on the pavement. If there is no stop line, stop at the crosswalk. If there is no crosswalk, stop at the edge of the sidewalk. If there is no sidewalk, stop at the edge of the intersection. Wait until the way is clear before entering the intersection.

 A school zone sign is five-sided and has a fluorescent yellow/green background with black symbols. It warns that you are coming to a school zone. Slow down, drive with extra caution and watch for children.

A yield sign is a triangle with a white background and a red border. It means you must let traffic in the intersection or close to it go first. Stop if necessary and go only when the way is clear.

A railway crossing sign is X-shaped with a white background and red outline. It warns that railway tracks cross the road. Watch for this sign. Slow down and look both ways for trains. Be prepared to stop.

There are four other kinds of signs: regulatory, warning, temporary conditions and information and direction.

Regulatory signs

These signs give a direction that must be obeyed. They are usually rectangular or square with a white or black background and black, white or coloured letters. A sign with a green circle means you may or must do the activity shown inside the ring. A red circle with a line through it means the activity shown is not allowed.

Here are some common regulatory signs:

This road is an official bicycle route. Watch for cyclists and be prepared to share the road with them.

You may park in the area between the signs during the times posted. (Used in pairs or groups.)

Snowmobiles may use this road.

Do not enter this road.

 Do not stop in the area between the signs. This means you may not stop your vehicle in this area, even for a moment. (Used in pairs or groups.)

 Do not stand in the area between the signs. This means you may not stop your vehicle in this area except while loading or unloading passengers. (Used in pairs or groups.)

 Do not park in the area between the signs. This means you may not stop your vehicle except to load or unload passengers or merchandise. (Used in pairs or groups.)

 Do not turn left at the intersection.

 Do not drive through the intersection.

 Do not turn to go in the opposite direction. (U-turn)

 Do not turn right when facing a red light at the intersection.

 Do not turn left during the times shown.

 This parking space is only for vehicles displaying a valid Accessible Parking Permit.

 No bicycles allowed on this road.

No pedestrians allowed on this road.

 Keep to the right of the traffic island.

 Speed limit changes ahead.

 Do not pass on this road.

 Slow traffic on multi-lane roads must keep right.

 Indicates areas where the community has identified that there is a special risk to pedestrians. Traffic related offences committed within the zone are subject to increased fines.

 The speed limit in this zone is lower during school hours. Observe the speed limit shown when the yellow lights are flashing.

   These signs, above the road or on the pavement before an intersection, tell drivers the direction they must travel. For example: the driver in lane one must turn left; the driver in lane two must turn left or go straight ahead; and the driver in lane three must turn right.

 Traffic may travel in one direction only.

  This is a pedestrian crossover. Be prepared to stop and yield right-of-way to pedestrians.

This sign, above the road or on the ground, means the lane is only for two-way left turns.

This sign reserves curb area for vehicles displaying a valid Accessible Parking Permit picking up and dropping off passengers with disabilities.

These signs mean lanes are only for specific types of vehicles, either all the time or during certain hours. Different symbols are used for the different types of vehicles. They include: buses, taxis, vehicles with three or more people and bicycles.

Keep to the right lane except when passing on two-lane sections where climbing or passing lanes are provided.

Stop for school bus when signals are flashing.

This sign is installed on multi-lane highways with no centre median divider. It informs drivers approaching from both directions that they must stop for a school bus when its signal lights are flashing.

 No trucks in this lane.

 No trucks over 6.5 metres in length in indicated lane.

 No trucks over 6.5 metres in length in this lane.

 Heavy trucks permitted on this roadway.

 Road forks to the right.

 No heavy trucks permitted on this roadway.

 No heavy trucks permitted on this roadway between the hours of 7 p.m. – 7 a.m.

 No vehicles over 10 tonnes on this roadway.

 No vehicles that bear more than five tonnes per axle permitted on this roadway.

 Indicates different weight restrictions for different types of heavy trucks for a bridge structure.

DANGEROUS GOODS ROUTE

Trucks carrying dangerous goods permitted on this roadway.

Trucks carrying dangerous goods permitted on this roadway.

Trucks carrying dangerous goods are not permitted on this roadway.

DANGEROUS GOODS CARRIERS PROHIBITED

No vehicles containing hazardous materials permitted on this roadway.

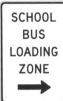

SCHOOL BUS LOADING ZONE

Marks a zone within which school buses load or unload passengers without using the red alternating lights and stop arm.

TRUCKS ENTER INSPECTION STATION
WHEN LIGHTS FLASHING

Trucks must enter inspection station when signals are flashing.

(407) ETR
Express Toll Route
Vehicles Over 5 Tonnes
Must Have Valid Transponder

Any trucks over five tonnes must have a valid 407 transponder to use ETR.

YIELD / **CÉDEZ**

This sign on the back of transit buses serves as a reminder to motorists of the law requiring vehicles approaching a bus stopped

at a dedicated Bus Stop to yield to the bus, once the bus has signalled its intent to return to the lane.

High Occupancy Vehicle (HOV) signs

2 or More Persons

Only public vehicles such as buses, or passenger vehicles carrying a specified minimum number of passengers, may use this lane.

Do Not Cross

Vehicles cannot change lanes into or out of a high-occupancy vehicle lane in this area.

Warning signs

These signs warn of dangerous or unusual conditions ahead such as a curve, turn, dip or sideroad. They are usually diamond-shaped and have a yellow background with black letters or symbols.

Here are some common warning signs:

Maximum vertical clearance of 3.9 metres.

Indicates that an upcoming structure might not allow room for a tall vehicle; therefore, drivers of such vehicles should choose an alternate route.

Trucks are advised to slow down around this curve due to its smaller radius.

Trucks over 10 tonnes are advised not to use this roadway.

Truck entrance on the right side of the road ahead. If the sign shows the truck on the left, the entrance is on the left side of the road.

Indicates an upcoming bus entrance on the right and vehicles should be aware of buses entering the roadway.

Indicates an upcoming fire truck entrance on the right and vehicles should be aware of fire trucks entering the roadway.

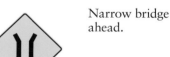

Narrow bridge ahead.

Road branching off ahead.

 Drivers on the side road at the intersection ahead don't have a clear view of traffic.

 Posted under a curve warning, this sign shows the maximum safe speed for the curve.

 Intersection ahead. The arrow shows which direction of traffic has the right-of-way.

 Pavement narrows ahead.

 Sharp bend or turn in the road ahead.

 Roundabout ahead. Reduce speed. The counter-clockwise arrows show the direction of vehicle traffic within the roundabout.

 Slight bend or curve in the road ahead.

 Chevron (arrowhead) signs are posted in groups to guide drivers around sharp curves in the road.

Winding road ahead.

 Bicycle crossing ahead.

 The share the road sign is used to warn motorists that they are to provide safe space on the road for cyclists and other vehicles.

 The bridge ahead lifts or swings to let boats pass.

 Stop sign ahead. Slow down.

 Pavement is slippery when wet. Slow down and drive with caution.

 Paved surface ends ahead.

 Share the road with oncoming traffic.

 Hazard close to the edge of the road. The downward lines show the side on which you may safely pass.

 Divided highway begins: traffic travels in both directions on separated roads ahead. Keep to the right-hand road. Each road carries one way traffic.

 Right lane ends ahead. If you are in the right-hand lane you must merge safely with traffic in the lane to the left.

 Traffic lights ahead. Slow down.

 Steep hill ahead. You may need to use a lower gear.

 Two roads going in the same direction are about to join into one. Drivers on both roads are equally responsible for seeing that traffic merges smoothly and safely.

 Snowmobiles cross this road.

 Divided highway ends: traffic travels in both directions on the same road ahead. Keep to the right-hand road.

 Bump or uneven pavement on the road ahead. Slow down and keep control of your vehicle.

Railway crossing ahead. Be alert for trains. This sign also shows the angle at which the railway tracks cross the road.

Shows maximum safe speed on ramp.

There may be water flowing over the road.

Sharp turn or bend in the road in the direction of the arrow. The checkerboard border warns of danger. Slow down; be careful.

Watch for pedestrians and be prepared to share the road with them.

This sign warns you that you are coming to a hidden school bus stop. Slow down, drive with extra caution, watch for children and for a school bus with flashing red lights.

Deer regularly cross this road; be alert for animals.

Watch for fallen rock and be prepared to avoid a collision.

These signs warn of a school crossing. Watch for children and follow the directions of the crossing guard or school safety patroller.

Temporary condition signs

These signs warn of unusual temporary conditions such as road work zones, diversions, detours, lane closures or traffic-control people on the road. They are usually diamond-shaped with an orange background and black letters or symbols.

Here are some common temporary condition signs:

Construction work one kilometre ahead.

Road work ahead.

Survey crew working on the road ahead.

Traffic control person ahead. Drive slowly and watch for instructions.

CONSTRUCTION ZONE BEGINS

You are entering a construction zone. Drive with extra caution and be prepared for a lower speed limit.

Temporary detour from normal traffic route.

Flashing lights on the arrows show the direction to follow.

Pavement has been milled or grooved. Your vehicle's stopping ability may be affected so obey the speed limit and drive with extra caution. Motorcyclists may experience reduced traction on these surfaces.

Lane ahead is closed for roadwork. Obey the speed limit and merge with traffic in the open lane.

Closed lane. Adjust speed to merge with traffic in lane indicated by arrow.

Do not pass the pilot or pace vehicle bearing this sign.

Reduce speed and be prepared to stop.

Follow detour marker until you return to regular route.

Enforces doubling the *HTA* fines for speeding in a designated construction zone when there are workers present.

Information and direction signs

These signs tell you about distances and destinations. They are usually rectangular with a green background and white letters. Other signs with different colours guide you to facilities, services and attractions.

Here are some common information and direction signs:

Shows directions to nearby towns and cities.

Shows the distances in kilometres to towns and cities on the road.

Various exit signs are used on freeways. In urban areas,

many exit ramps have more than one lane. Overhead and ground-mounted signs help drivers choose the correct lane to exit or stay on the freeway.

 Advance signs use arrows to show which lanes lead off the freeway. Signs are also posted at the exit.

 Sometimes one or more lanes may lead off the freeway. The arrows matching the exit lanes are shown on the advance sign in a yellow box with the word 'exit' under them.

 Freeway interchanges or exits have numbers that correspond to the distance from the beginning of the freeway. For example, interchange number 204 on Highway 401 is 204 kilometres from Windsor, where the freeway begins. Distances can be calculated by subtracting one interchange number from another.

The term "VIA" is used to describe the roads that must be followed to reach a destination.

Shows the upcoming roundabout exists and where they will take you.

These signs change according to traffic conditions to give drivers current information on delays and lane closures ahead.

Shows off-road facilities such as hospitals, airports, universities or carpool lots.

Shows route to passenger railway station.

Shows route to airport.

Shows route to ferry service.

Shows facilities that are accessible by wheelchair.

Other signs

Here are some other common signs:

Oversize load sign

Vehicles and/or loads in excess of dimensions prescribed under Section 109 of the *Highway Traffic Act* must be marked with bright red or orange warning flags, which are at least 40 cm square, mounted to the extremities of the vehicle or load. The flag(s) must be kept in good and clean condition so as to not diminish their effectiveness.

In addition to flags, vehicles and/or loads must display on the front of the vehicle and the rear of the load, in a clearly visible position, either one of the two following signs: a sign visible for a distance of at least 150 metres bearing the words "OVERSIZE LOAD" in black letters at least 200 millimetres high on a yellow background; or, a "D" sign, as illustrated. When travelling at night, the sign must be made of high-intensity, retro-reflective material. The sign cannot obstruct lights or other safety devices on the vehicle or trailer; and it must be removed or covered when not in use.

The following is a diagram of a "D" sign.

Long commercial vehicle (LCV)

This placard indicates a long commercial vehicle, which is a double trailer and can be up to 40 metres in length. It is important to be able to recognize an LCV on the highway, based on rear signage, and anticipate both extended length and limited speed when preparing to pass one on the highway.

Slow-moving vehicle sign

The "slow-moving vehicle" sign is an orange triangle with a red border. It alerts other drivers that this vehicle will be travelling at 40 km/h or less. When on a road, farm tractors, farm implements/machinery and vehicles not capable of sustaining speeds over 40 km/h must display the slow moving vehicle sign. Watch for these slow moving vehicles and reduce your speed as necessary.

Dangerous goods

When transporting dangerous goods, safety marks, placards or labels are displayed to identify dangerous-

goods classification and the nature of danger they pose. They are an information tool to provide a quick identification that can be found on

trucks, cargo and even pallets. EDR signs are used during the unscheduled closure of a provincial highway when OPP detour all traffic off the highway. The EDR markers are located along alternative routes and provide direction to motorists around the closure and back onto the highway.

Emergency response signs

Some information signs include a numbering system along the bottom of the sign to assist emergency vehicles and drivers in determining an appropriate route.

Bilingual signs

Watch for these signs when driving in designated bilingual areas. Read the messages in the language you understand best. Bilingual messages may be together on the same sign or separate, with an English sign immediately followed by a French sign.

II. TRAFFIC LIGHTS

Traffic lights tell drivers and pedestrians what they must do at intersections and along roads. They tell road users when to stop and go, when and how to turn and when to drive with extra caution.

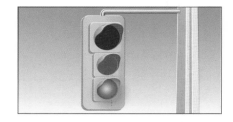

Green light

A green light means you may turn left, go straight or turn right after yielding to vehicles and pedestrians already in the intersection. When turning left or right you must yield the right-of-way to pedestrians crossing the intersection.

Yellow light

A yellow — or amber — light means the red light is about to appear. You must stop if you can do so safely; otherwise, go with caution.

Red light

A red light means you must stop. Bring your vehicle to a complete stop at the stop line if it is marked on the pavement. If there is no stop line, stop at the crosswalk, marked or not. If there is no crosswalk, stop at the edge of the sidewalk. If there is no sidewalk, stop at the edge of the intersection.

Wait until the light changes to green and the intersection is clear before moving through it.

Unless a sign tells you not to, you may turn right on a red light only after coming to a complete stop and waiting until the way is clear. You may also turn left on a red light if you are moving from a one-way road onto a one-way road, but you must come to a complete stop first and wait until the way is clear.

Lights and arrows to help turning vehicles

Flashing green lights and green arrows direct drivers who are turning.

Advance green light or arrow

When you face a flashing green light or a left-pointing green arrow and a green light, you may turn left, go straight ahead or turn right from the proper lane. This is called an advanced green light because oncoming traffic still faces a red light.

Pedestrians must not cross on a flashing green light unless a pedestrian signal tells them to.

Simultaneous left turn

When a left-turn green arrow is shown with a red light, you may turn left from the left-turn lane. Vehicles turning left from the opposite direction may also be making left turns because they too face a left-turn green arrow.

After the left-turn green arrow, a yellow arrow may appear. This means the green light is about to appear for traffic in one or both directions. Do not start your left turn. Stop if you can do so safely; otherwise, complete your turn with caution.

You can still turn left when the light is green, but only when the way is clear of traffic and pedestrians. If the light turns red when you are in the intersection, complete your turn when it is safe.

Pedestrians must not cross on a left-turn green arrow unless a pedestrian signal tells them to.

Transit priority signals

Traffic and pedestrians must yield to public transit vehicles at a transit priority signal. The round signal is on top of a regular traffic signal and shows a white vertical bar on a dark background. This allows transit vehicles to go through, turn right or left, while all conflicting traffic faces a red light.

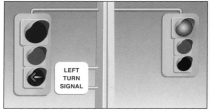

Fully protected left turn

Some intersections have separate traffic lights for left-turning traffic and for traffic going through the intersection or turning right.

When a left-turn green arrow appears for traffic in the left-turn lane, traffic going straight ahead or turning right will usually see a red light. You may turn left from the left-turn lane when you face a green arrow. Vehicles from the opposite direction may also be turning left.

After the left-turn green arrow, a yellow light appears for left-turning vehicles only.

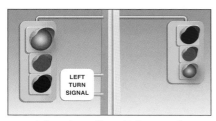

After the yellow light, a red light appears for left-turning vehicles only. Traffic going straight ahead or turning right will face a green light or green arrows pointing straight ahead and to the right.

In these intersections, you may not begin turning left after the green light appears for traffic going straight ahead or turning right. If the light turns yellow while you are in the intersection, complete your turn with caution.

Flashing red light

You must come to a complete stop at a flashing red light. Move through the intersection only when it is safe.

Flashing yellow light

A flashing yellow light means you should drive with caution when approaching and moving through the intersection.

Blank traffic lights

During an electrical power loss, traffic lights at intersections will not work. Yield the right-of-way to vehicles in the intersection and to vehicles entering the intersection from your right. Go cautiously and use the intersection the same way you would use an intersection with all-way stop signs.

Traffic beacons

A traffic beacon is a single flashing light hung over an intersection or placed over signs or on obstacles in the road.

Flashing red beacon

A flashing red beacon above an intersection or stop sign means you must come to a complete stop. Move through the intersection only when it is safe to do so.

Flashing yellow beacon

A flashing yellow beacon above an intersection, above a warning sign or on an obstruction in the road, warns you to drive with caution.

III. PEDESTRIAN SIGNALS

Pedestrian signals help pedestrians cross at intersections with traffic lights. The signal for pedestrians to walk is a white walking symbol. A flashing or steady orange hand symbol means pedestrians must not begin to cross.

A pedestrian facing a walk signal may cross the road in the direction of the signal. While crossing, pedestrians have the right-of-way over all vehicles.

A pedestrian facing a flashing or steady hand symbol should not begin to cross the road. Pedestrians who have already begun to cross when the hand signal appears, should go as quickly as possible to a safe area. While they are crossing, pedestrians still have the right-of-way over vehicles.

At intersections with traffic lights where there are no pedestrian signals, pedestrians facing a green light may cross. Pedestrians may not cross on a flashing green light or a left-turn green arrow.

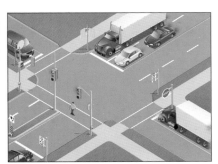

Intersection pedestrian signals

Where there are pedestrian push buttons, a pedestrian must use the button to bring on the walk signal. Pedestrian signals give people more time to cross than regular traffic lights. On a busy main road, an intersection pedestrian signal helps people to cross the road safely by signalling traffic to stop. The intersection pedestrian signal has one or more crosswalks; pedestrian walk and don't walk signals; push buttons for pedestrians; and, traffic signal lights on the main road only. Stop signs control traffic on the smaller, less busy crossroad.

You must observe, obey the traffic rules and use safe driving skills to drive through these intersections. (See Yielding the right-of-way on page 49.)

IV. PAVEMENT MARKINGS

Pavement markings combine with road signs and traffic lights to give you important information about the direction of traffic and where you may and may not travel. Pavement markings divide traffic lanes, show turning lanes, mark pedestrian crossings, indicate obstacles and tell you when it is not safe to pass.

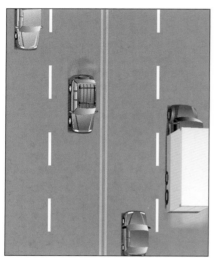

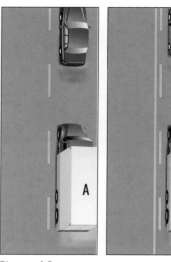

Diagram 4-1

Yellow lines separate traffic travelling in opposite directions. White lines separate traffic travelling in the same direction.

Diagram 4-2

A solid line at the left of your lane means it is unsafe to pass. ("A" should not pass.)

Diagram 4-3

A broken line at the left of your lane means you may pass if the way is clear. ("A" may pass if there are enough broken lines ahead to complete the pass safely.)

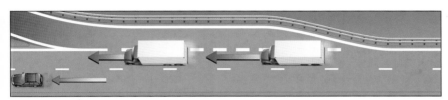

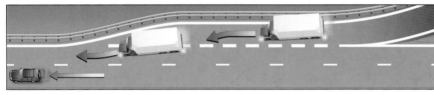

Diagram 4-5

Diagram 4-4

Broken lines that are wider and closer together than regular broken lines are called continuity lines. When you see continuity lines on your left side, it means the lane you are in is ending or exiting, and that you must change lanes if you want to continue in your current direction. Continuity lines on your right mean your lane will continue unaffected.

A stop line is a single white line painted across the road at an intersection. It shows where you must stop. If there is no stop line marked on the road, stop at the crosswalk, marked or not. If there is no crosswalk, stop at the edge of the sidewalk. If there is no sidewalk, stop at the edge of the (Diagram 4-5) intersection.

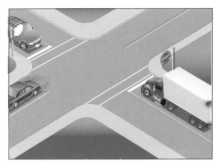

Diagram 4-6

A crosswalk is marked by two parallel white lines painted across the road. However, crosswalks at intersections are not always marked. If there is no stop line, stop at the crosswalk. If there is no crosswalk, stop at the edge of the sidewalk. If there is no sidewalk, stop at the edge of the intersection.

Diagram 4-7

A white arrow painted on a lane means you may move only in the direction of the arrow.

Diagram 4-8

A pedestrian crossover is marked by two white double parallel lines across the road with an X in each lane approaching it, and overhead yellow lights. Stop before the line and yield to pedestrians.

Diagram 4-9

Two solid lines painted on the pavement guide traffic away from fixed objects such as bridge piers or concrete islands.

Yellow and black markings are also painted on the objects themselves as warnings.

Chapter 4-Summary

By the end of this chapter you should know:

Signs

- The difference between regulatory, warning, temporary condition and information/ direction signs
- How to read the symbols and messages of some common signs in each category

Traffic Lights

- The different colours and symbols that appear on traffic lights and what those mean
- How to navigate turns using advanced green lights and arrows
- How to proceed when approaching flashing amber or red lights
- What to do in situations where the traffic lights are not operating

Pedestrian Signals

- What the symbols on pedestrian signals indicate
- What an intersection pedestrian signal is and what to do if you encounter one

Pavement Markings

- How pavement markings are used to control traffic
- What the different colours and types of markings are used to indicate

CHAPTER 5
KEEPING YOUR LICENCE

I. KEEPING YOUR LICENCE

Ontario has a one-piece driver's licence. The licence card has a photograph and signature of the driver. All drivers in Ontario should have a one-piece licence card. You must carry your licence with you whenever you drive.

Renewing your licence

When your licence is due for renewal, you will get a renewal application form either via e-mail or mail. Drivers under the age of 80 with class A, B, C, E or F and drivers over the age of 65 with a class D licence must pass a vision and knowledge test in order to renew their licence usually every five years.

Effective July 1, 2018, requirements for class D drivers under the age of 65 have changed. Drivers under age 65 will be required to pass a vision test and knowledge test in order to renew their licence.

Drivers aged 65 to 79 with class A, B, C, D, E or F licences are required to pass a vision, knowledge and road test in the event of an at-fault collision or the accumulation of three or more demerit points. For those commercial drivers with an air brake endorsement, the written air brake test has been aligned with the written knowledge test cycle, and the practical air brake test is only required when a road test is triggered. Drivers 80 and over with Class A, B, C, D, E or F licences are required to pass a vision, knowledge and road test prior to renewing their licence.

Commercial-class licence holders, depending on their age, are required to periodically submit a satisfactory medical report to maintain their commercial licence, or otherwise be downgraded to a Class G licence (refer to Medical Reporting). Effective July 1, 2018 class D drivers will also be required to periodically submit and pass a medical report to maintain their class D licence, or otherwise be downgraded to a class G licence.

If any tests are required, you must attend a DriveTest Centre to complete the tests and renew your licence. If no tests are required, you must renew your licence in person at any ServiceOntario centre. Take the form into any ServiceOntario centre in the province. They are all equipped to take photographs. You will be asked to sign the form, show identification, pay a fee and have your photograph taken. You will get a temporary licence on the spot if your application and documents are in order, and your permanent one will be mailed to you. You must carry it with you whenever you drive, and produce it when a police officer requests it.

If you do not get a renewal application form in the mail when your licence is due for renewal, call the Ministry of Transportation. You are responsible for making sure you have a valid driver's licence.

If your licence has been suspended, cancelled or expired for more than three years, you will be required to re-apply for a licence in Ontario and meet all the requirements of graduated licensing, including passing all the required tests. Only then will you be eligible to re-apply for any commercial-class licences.

Medical reporting

If you have any commercial vehicle driver's licence other than a class D licence, you must pass a medical examination every one to five years, depending on your age. You will get a notice and a blank medical-report form in the mail three months before your medical report is due. You must go to a doctor and get a medical examination. The doctor completes

Reason For Name Change	Documentation Required
Marriage	Government-Issued Marriage Certificate Change-of-Name Certificate
Common Law Alliance	Change-of-Name Certificate
Adoption	Court Order for Adoption Change-of-Name Certificate
Under the *Change-of-Name Act*	Change-of-Name Certificate

the form. You must submit the form to the Ministry of Transportation, either by mail or in person. If you do not file a medical report, your class of licence will be downgraded.

- Drivers under the age of 46 are required to submit a medical report every five years.
- Drivers aged 46 to 64 are required to submit a medical report every three years.
- Drivers aged 65 or older are required to submit a medical report every year.
- Drivers aged 80 and older with a class D licence must submit a medical report every year.

Changing your name or address

You must tell the Ministry of Transportation within six days of changing your name or address. You will need a new licence when you change your address. You can change your address on the ServiceOntario website at www.serviceontario.ca, or you can take the change of information to a ServiceOntario centre, or mail it to the Ministry of Transportation, P.O. Box 9200, Kingston, ON K7L 5K4. The ministry will send you a new licence. When you get it, destroy your old licence and carry the new one with you whenever you drive.

If you change your name, you need a new licence. Take the documents you must show and your current licence to a ServiceOntario centre. A new photograph will be taken.

You will get a temporary licence to use until your permanent licence is mailed to you. Carry it with you whenever you drive.

There is no charge for getting a new licence because you change your name or address.

The chart on the previous page shows the documents you will need to change your name on your driver's licence.

Driver's licence laws

It is illegal to:
- Lend your licence
- Let someone else use it
- Use an altered licence
- Use another licence as your own
- Have more than one Ontario driver's licence
- Use a fictitious or imitation licence

II. THE DEMERIT POINT SYSTEM

The demerit point system encourages drivers to improve their behaviour and protects people from drivers who abuse the privilege of driving. Drivers convicted of driving-related offences have demerit points recorded on their records. Demerit points stay on your record for two years from the date of the offence. If you accumulate too many demerit points, your driver's licence can be suspended.

III. OTHER WAYS TO LOSE YOUR LICENCE

Your licence may also be suspended for the following reasons:

Medical suspension

By law, all doctors must report the names and addresses of everyone 16 years or older who has any condition that may affect their ability to drive safely (for examlple, a stroke, heart condition or dizziness). Doctors report this information to the Ministry of Transportation, and it is not given to anyone else. Your driver's licence may be suspended until new medical evidence shows that the condition does not pose a safety risk.

Zero tolerance for commercial drivers

Drivers of commercial vehicles must not have any presence of alcohol and/or a drug in their system when driving a commercial vehicle. If a commercial driver has alcohol or a drug in their system, they will face serious penalties, including licence suspensions and administrative monetary penalties.

Commercial vehicle drivers (classes A to F) have a zero-tolerance sanction for drugs and alcohol impairment when behind the wheel of these types of vehicles:
- Those that require a class A to F licence
- One requiring a Commercial Vehicle Operator's Registration (CVOR)
- Road-building machine

If police determine that you have the presence of drugs or alcohol in your system and/or that you are impaired by any substance including illegal drugs, prescription drugs or over-the-counter medications, you will face severe consequences, including potential criminal charges and jail time.

Impaired driving

Driving when your ability is impaired by alcohol or a drug, is a crime in Canada. Your vehicle does not even have to be moving; you can be charged if you are impaired behind the wheel, even if you have not started to drive. In circumstances involving possible impairment by a drug or a combination of alcohol and a drug, police can require a driver to:
- provide breath samples
- perform standardized field sobriety tests
- conduct a drug-recognition evaluation
- provide oral fluid urine or blood samples for screening.

If you fail or refuse to comply with any of these demands, you will be charged under the Criminal Code.

If you are 21 years of age and under, you must not drive if you have been drinking alcohol. Your blood alcohol level must be zero.

For more information on impaired driving measures in Ontario, please visit the Ministry of Transportation website at: http://www.mto.gov.on.ca/english/safety/impaired-driving.shtml

Alcohol

The police can stop any driver to determine if alcohol or drug testing is required. They may also do roadside spot checks. When stopped by the police, you may be told to blow into a machine that tests your breath for alcohol, a roadside screening device, or perform physical co-ordination tests. If you fail, are unable or refuse to provide a breath sample or to perform the physical co-ordination tests, you will be charged under the Criminal Code.

If you cannot give a breath sample or it is impractical to obtain a sample of breath, the police officer can require you to provide a blood sample instead.

Drugs

The police can stop any driver to determine if drug testing is required. Criminal Code and *HTA* sanctions apply to drivers impaired by alcohol or a drug.

Drugs in all forms, including cannabis, illegal drugs, prescription drugs or over-the-counter medications, can have dangerous effects:
- If you use prescription medicines or get allergy shots, ask your doctor about side effects such as dizziness, blurred vision, nausea or drowsiness that could affect your driving.
- Read the information on the package of any over-the-counter medicine you take. Any stimulant, diet pill, tranquillizer or sedative may affect your driving. Even allergy and cold remedies may have ingredients that could affect your driving.

- Drugs and alcohol together can have dangerous effects, even several days after you have taken the drug.

Do not take a chance; ask your doctor or pharmacist before you drive.

Chapter 5-Summary

By the end of this chapter you should know:

- Your responsibility to maintain a valid driver's licence with the most correct and up-to-date information
- How the demerit point system works for fully licensed drivers
- Common circumstances where your licence can be cancelled or suspended
- How alcohol and drugs affect your ability to drive

CHAPTER 6
ROAD TEST

As part of the Class A or D road test, you will be required:

1. Through the Daily Inspection test, to determine the safe operation of the vehicle, and identify any of the prescribed minor or major defects as listed in the applicable schedules in the Regulation. O. Reg. 199/07.
2. Through the Backing Skills test, to display backing skills essential for the safe control of the vehicle while reversing into a desired location and simultaneously judging the vehicle's position as it relates to surrounding objects.
3. Through the On-Road Driving test, to display skills required to drive a commercial vehicle in most traffic situations while obeying all relevant signs, signals and rules of the road.

The Class A and D road test is made up of the following components.

1. Daily inspection test:
- Exterior inspection
- In-cab check
- Interior inspection

Uncoupling and coupling (Class A)

2. Backing skills test:
- Offset backing–left or right, OR
- Alley dock (90-degree backing)

3. On-road driving test:
- Left and right turns
- Intersections
- Lane changes
- Driving along
- Expressway section
- Curves
- Roadside stop/start

Pre-test requirements

For all Class A (including Class AR) and any Class D road test where the vehicle is equipped with air brakes, you must bring the following:

- Wheel chocks or blocks
- Means of keeping time to measure seconds
- A means of holding the brake pedal in the applied position
- A device for measuring pushrod stroke

If you do not have all of the listed items, the road test will be declared out of order, and you must pay 50 per cent of the road-test fee before you may reschedule the next road test.

Note: Protective headgear/eyewear, a chart of brake-adjustment limits and a means of marking the pushrod (chalk or similar) are recommended items, but not mandatory.

Daily inspection report and applicable schedule

- Prior to the road test, you must provide the examiner with a valid and completed daily inspection report, as well as the applicable schedule relative to your vehicle.

Inspection stickers

- You must also ensure your vehicle has the appropriate annual inspection stickers or valid paper copies.

DAILY INSPECTION TEST
Introduction and overview

The purpose of the daily inspection test is to determine if you have the knowledge and skills required for the safe operation of the vehicle and to identify any of the prescribed minor or major defects as listed in the applicable schedule(s) in the Ontario Regulation. O. Reg.199/07.

The daily inspection test is divided into the following sections and will be performed in the following order:

1. Exterior inspection
2. In-cab check
3. Interior inspection

The exterior and interior portions of the daily inspection test will be administered using a random selection of testing items from Schedule 1 in Regulation O. Reg. 199/07. This will ensure that you are prepared to inspect all components of the vehicle.

You will be required to inspect all items listed for the in-cab portion of the test. You will be permitted to use Schedule 1 as a guide and reference during the daily inspection test.

Exterior inspection

The exterior inspection of the vehicle must be performed with the parking brake engaged (for all Class A vehicles and vehicles equipped with air brakes, unless when necessary to release the parking brake during the course of the inspection) and the wheels chocked.

You will be asked to find and inspect four randomly generated items from the list below and be required to:

- Demonstrate and describe how you would inspect the particular item.
- Explain what the defect(s) would be for the particular item.
- Describe what action you would take upon identifying a minor and/or major defect.

For all full Class A road tests and any road test where the vehicle is equipped with air brakes, you must be prepared to inspect any of the air brake components of the vehicle listed below, as well as any of the other items. The list also provides inspection methods for each item.

Exterior items:
1. Slow air pressure build-up rate
You must know the proper method for testing the air pressure build-up rate, and that a vehicle has this minor defect when it takes longer than two minutes for air pressure to build up from 85 to 100 psi.

Procedure:
- Ensure the trailer supply valve is closed (pulled out when equipped).
- Release the parking brake.
- Pump brakes to reduce air pressure to 552 kPa (80 psi or less).
- Maintain engine speed of 600 to 900 r.p.m.
- Note time for pressure to rise from 587 to 690 kPa (85 to 100 psi) while maintaining specified engine speed.
- Note the build-up time and tell the examiner.

2. Audible air leaks
You must know that it's necessary to check for leaks regularly, and a vehicle has this minor defect when any air leak can be heard.

Air-loss rate exceeds the prescribed limit
You must know the proper method for testing the air-loss rate, and that a vehicle has this major defect when the air pressure drops in one minute more than the prescribed limit of:
- 28 kPa (4 psi) in one minute for Class A
- 21 kPa (3 psi) in one minute for Class D

Procedure:
- Tell the examiner, "For any air leaks heard at any time, I would conduct the air-loss rate test."
- Ensure the vehicle is secured by wheel chocks.
- Release all spring parking/emergency brakes.
- Ensure the air-system pressure is between cut-in and cut-out values (80 -145 psi); shut off the engine and turn the key on (if required).
- Hold the brake pedal in the fully applied position.
- Observe the air pressure gauges for one minute and note any change. (Disregard the initial pressure drop and begin test after the pressure has stabilized.)

3. Pushrod stroke of any brake exceeds the adjustment limit

You must know the proper method for checking brake pushrod stroke, and that a vehicle has this major defect when the pushrod stroke of any brake is longer than the prescribed limit.

Certain vehicles do not provide access to measure the applied pushrod stroke (buses, low-slung vehicles and those with obstructive fairing or body panels, or vehicles equipped with air disk brakes). In such cases, the examination is conducted verbally.

Here are the steps you must take to measure applied pushrod stroke.

1. Secure the vehicle with wheel chocks or blocks.
2. Ensure air pressure is above 621 kPa (90 psi) and release the spring brakes.
3. Select one of the following methods:

- **Method 1:** Mark the pushrod at the brake chamber or at a suitable fixed reference point. (Use chalk, soapstone, marker or other similar instrument. Marks must be narrow and precise.)
- **Method 2:** Measure the released position of the pushrod. (Measure and note the distance from a point on the pushrod to a suitable fixed point at the brake chamber. This is measurement number 1.)

4. Raise or lower the air pressure by running the engine or pumping the brake pedal until both the primary and secondary air-tank gauges display 621 to 690 kPa (90 to 100 psi).
5. Shut off the engine.
6. Press and hold the brake pedal in the fully applied position, and use a suitable means to hold the brakes applied in order to leave the cab and inspect them.
7. Determine the applied pushrod stroke. (Continue to use the previously selected method.)

- **Method 1:** Measure the distance from the brake chamber or fixed reference point to the mark on the pushrod.
- **Method 2:** Measure the applied position of the pushrod. (Remeasure and note the distance from the previously selected point on the pushrod to the previously selected fixed point at the brake chamber. This is measurement number 2.) Subtract measurement 1 from measurement 2 to calculate the applied pushrod stroke measurement.

8. Determine and indicate the number size (such as 16, 20, 24 or 30) and type (such as standard or long-stroke) of the brake chamber.
9. Determine and indicate the adjustment limit for the brake chamber.
10. Compare the applied pushrod stroke to the applicable adjustment limit and identify any brake that exceeds the adjustment limit as defective.

4. Inoperative towing vehicle (tractor) protection valve

You must know the proper method for testing the tractor (towing vehicle) protections system, and that a vehicle has this major defect when air escapes from the service line during service-brake application, when the trailer supply valve is closed.

Procedure:

- Ensure air pressure is within its normal operating pressure range, cut-in and cut-out values (80 -145 psi).
- Ensure the trailer supply valve is closed (pulled out).
- Remove the trailer service-line coupler (glad-hand) from the trailer or its storage location, and place it where it can be observed.
- Apply service brakes.

Note: If you are concerned that the vehicle has no anti-compounding valve, you must ensure the vehicle is secure and release the spring (parking/emergency) brakes before applying the service brakes.

- Observe if any air is exhausting from the trailer service-line coupler (glad-hand).

5. Low-air warning system fails or system is activated

You must know the proper method for testing the low-air warning, and that a vehicle has this major defect when the low-air warning fails to activate or activates before air pressure drops below 55 psi.

Procedure:

- Ensure air pressure is above 621 kPa (90 psi). If air pressure is too low, warning may activate as soon as ignition key is turned on.
- Ensure ignition key is turned on. Engine may be running or shut off. (If ignition key is not turned on, the warning will not activate.)
- Press and release the brake pedal (to lower pressure) several times until warning activates.

- Watch the pressure gauges and note the pressure when the low-air warning device activates. (Low-air warning device may only be a light, or a light and an audible device.)

6. Occupant compartment door fails to open

You must know that the occupant, driver and passenger doors must be able to open in an emergency, and that a vehicle has this minor defect when any door meant for someone to enter or exit the cab fails to open.

Any cab or sleeper door fails to close securely

You must know that the driver, passenger or occupant door must remain securely closed when a vehicle is moving, and that a vehicle has this major defect when any door meant for someone to enter or exit the cab fails to close securely.

Procedure:

- Test the function of the selected door to ensure the door opens properly and closes securely.

7. Coupler or mounting has loose or missing fastener

You must know that the condition of couplers and the mounting structure need to be inspected visually, and that a vehicle has this minor defect when any coupler or the mounting structure that supports a coupler has a fastener that is loose or missing.

Procedure:

- Physically check and verbally describe the coupler assembly (for example, fifth wheel or pintle hook) and the related mounting fasteners.
- Point and check for loose and missing fasteners.
- Point out the fasteners to the examiner.

8. Coupler is insecure or movement exceeds prescribed limit

You must know the symptoms of couplers that are loose or are developing abnormal amounts of movement, methods for measuring the amount of movement or having it measured, and that a vehicle has this major defect when:

a) Movement between the upper and lower coupler of a fifth wheel is more than 1/2 in. (13mm) in the forward/rearward direction.

b) Movement between the pintle hook and a drawbar eye is more than 3/8 in. (10mm) in the forward/rearward direction.

Procedure:

- Position yourself to be able to see the coupler assembly and the related mounting structure and attachments.
- Visually check for evidence of damaged, broken, cracked, loose or missing components.
- State what is being checked.
- Apply trailer brakes and release tractor brakes.
- Verbally state when in or after coupling, "I will feel for excessive play/movement."
- Verbally describe the process to check and measure coupler movement: tractor trailer combination only.
- Apply trailer brakes and, using the power train, gently pull tractor as far forward as possible.
- Mark the fifth wheel with chalk or similar marking.
- Use the power train to move the tractor rearward against the trailer as far as possible.
- Observe the distance between the markings placed on the fifth wheel and confirm it is less than 1/2 in. (13 mm) for fifth wheel or 3/8 in. (10 mm) for pintle hook.

9. Coupling or locking mechanism is damaged or fails to lock

You must know the importance of having couplers properly locked, the locking methods used by couplers, how to visually inspect these locks, and also know that a vehicle has this major defect when any coupler or lock is damaged or isn't properly locked.

Procedure:
Fifth-wheel couplers:

- Position yourself to be able to see the coupler assembly.
- Visually verify the position of the fifth-wheel release handle.
- Visually check the position of any exposed mechanism on the fifth wheel.
- Describe the following procedure. Get under the trailer at the rear of the tractor and visually inspect the position of the fifth-wheel locking jaws.

Pintle-hook couplers:

- Position yourself to be able to see the coupler assembly.
- Visually check the position and condition of the latching and locking mechanism.

10. Defective, incorrect or missing safety chain/cable

You must know the importance of safety chains and cables, the type that must be used, as well as the condition they need to be in, and that a vehicle has this major defect when a safety chain or cable is missing, is the wrong type or size, or is noticeably damaged or worn out.

Procedure:

- Inspect the safety chain(s) to ensure they are hooked and crossed (when two chains), and hooks are secured with a secondary hook.

11. Exhaust system

Exhaust leak

- You must know how to visually inspect the exhaust system, and that a vehicle has this minor defect when there's a noticeable exhaust leak.

Exhaust leak that causes exhaust gas to enter the occupant compartment

- You must know the hazard of prolonged exposure to engine exhaust gases, and that the vehicle has this major defect when exhaust gases from an exhaust-system leak are getting into the cab.

Procedure:

- With the vehicle running, open the hood or other compartments as required, and inspect the complete exhaust system to ensure there are no signs of exhaust leaks.

12. Damaged frame or cargo body

You must know that the condition of the vehicle and any cargo body frame need to be inspected visually, and that a vehicle has this minor defect when there's any noticeable or suspected damage such as a cracked, bent or deformed part or section in the frame or cargo body.

Visibly shifted, cracked, collapsing or sagging frame member(s)
You must know that some conditions of the frame or cargo body can be very serious safety concerns, and that a vehicle has this major defect when it is visible, when any frame component has shifted, is cracked, collapsing or sagging.

Procedure:
• Inspect one side of the vehicle and open hood to check for any noticeable or suspected damage such as a cracked, bent or deformed part or section in the frame or cargo body, or any frame component has shifted, is cracked, collapsing or sagging.

13. Fuel systems
Missing fuel tank cap
You must know the hazards of fuel spillage and fuel contamination, and that a vehicle has this minor defect when the fuel-tank cap is missing.

Insecure fuel tank
You must know that fuel tanks must be securely attached to a vehicle and how to visually inspect fuel-tank security, and that a vehicle has this major defect when a fuel tank isn't securely mounted or otherwise attached to the vehicle.

Dripping fuel leak
You must know the hazards of fuel that is flammable and an environmental hazard, and that a vehicle has this major defect when there is fuel dripping anywhere from it.

Procedure:
Visually inspect to ensure:
• Fuel cap(s) are not missing.

• Fuel tank(s) are secure; where accessible, inspect straps to ensure they are attached (not required to grab or shake fuel tank or straps).
• Fuel is not leaking from the fuel tank(s) or dripping from anywhere from the vehicle including under engine compartment and fuel tanks.

14. Glass and mirrors
Required mirror or glass has broken or damaged attachments onto vehicle body
You must know that the windows and mirrors that are necessary for safe operation must also be securely attached to vehicle, and that the vehicle has this minor defect when the attachments for any required mirror or other glass are broken or damaged.

Procedure:
• Inspect the vehicle to ensure all external mirrors and mirror attachments onto the vehicle body are secure, not broken or damaged.

15. Hydraulic brake system

Brake fluid level is below indicated minimum level and brake fluid reservoir is less than one-quarter full

You must know the location of the hydraulic brake master-cylinder reservoir, how to check the level of the brake fluid, and that the vehicle has this minor defect when the brake fluid level is below the mark indicating the minimum level as determined by the manufacturer, or a major defect when the reservoir is less than one-quarter full.

Brake fluid leak

You must know that brake fluid is required for the system to operate, that loss of brake fluid can cause the brakes to malfunction or fail completely, and that a vehicle has this major defect when a brake fluid leak is noticeable.

Procedure:

Open the hood and inspect brake-fluid reservoirs to ensure:

- Brake fluid is above the minimum required level.
- There is no brake-fluid leak.
- Brake-fluid reservoir is not less than one-quarter full.

16. Suspension system

Air leak in air-suspension system

You must know that a vehicle has a minor defect when an air leak is noticeable in the air-suspension system.

Damaged (patched, cut, bruised, cracked to braid or deflated) air bag

You must know the normal appearance of air bags used in vehicle suspension systems, be able to recognize the signs of damage and identify when the damage may also cause an air bag to be deflated. You must also know a vehicle has a major defect when any air bag is damaged and has no air in it.

Procedure:

- Inspect the vehicle (or describes the process) to ensure an air leak is

not noticeable in the air-suspension system and any air bag is not damaged and has air in it.

17. Suspension system

Broken leaf spring

You must know the importance of doing a visual inspection of leaf springs and how to identify a broken leaf spring, and that the vehicle has this minor defect when any spring has a single broken leaf.

Cracked or broken main spring leaf or more than one broken leaf spring

You must know which leaves in a spring are considered to be "main" leaves, and that a vehicle has this major defect when either a main leaf or more than one other leaf is broken.

Part of leaf spring or suspension is missing, shifted out of place, in contact with another vehicle component

You must know the condition of the suspension-system components, and the hardware that attaches it to the vehicle need to be inspected visually; you must be able to recognize the signs of more serious unsafe suspension-system conditions, and that a vehicle has this major defect when any part of a leaf spring or suspension part is missing, has shifted out of place or is in contact with another vehicle component.

Procedure:

- Inspect the vehicle (or describe the process where not accessible) to identify any cracked or broken spring leaves, or a spring leaf or suspension part is missing, has shifted out of place or is in contact with another vehicle component.

18. Suspension system

Suspension fastener is loose, missing or broken
You must know the condition of the suspension-system components and the hardware that attaches it to the vehicle need to be inspected visu-

ally; you must be able to recognize the signs of loose, missing or broken components, and also know that a vehicle has this minor defect when any suspension fastener is loose, missing or broken.

Loose u-bolt
You must know how to locate and identify suspension U-bolts, know the importance of ensuring they remain tight, as well as the signs of loose U-bolts. You must also know that a vehicle has this major defect when any spring U-bolt is loose.

Procedure:

- Inspect the condition of the suspension-system components and the hardware, including suspension fasteners and U-bolts, that attaches it to the vehicle for any visual signs of loose, missing or broken components.

19. Tires - leaks

Tire leaking, if leak cannot be heard
You must know the importance of keeping tires properly inflated, appreciate the need to regularly check for leaks, and that a vehicle has this minor defect when a leak appears evident, but cannot be felt or heard in any tire.

Tire flat, if leak can be felt or heard
You must know the dangers of operating with a flat tire, and that a vehicle has this major defect when any tire is flat, or when a leak can be felt or heard.

Procedure:

- Select one tire of the vehicle and inspect tire for any leaks (listen and feel).

Note: Kicking the tires or using a mallet to check for flats is acceptable.

20. Tires - damage and tread
Damaged tread or sidewall of tire
You must be able to distinguish between the tread and sidewall of a tire, recognizing the visual signs of damage to them, and know that a vehicle has this minor defect when there is damage to the tread or sidewall area.

Tire-tread depth is less than wear limit
You must know how to check tire-tread depth and the minimum allowable depth for various tire positions in vehicle safety regulations, and that a vehicle has this major defect when any tire's tread depth is below the allowable wear limit.

Tire is in contact with another tire or any vehicle component other than mud flap
You must know that tires should never contact other vehicle components, and while a tire contacting a mud flap is not a safety concern, that a vehicle has this major defect when any tire is in contact with another tire or any other vehicle component.

Tire has exposed cords in the tread or outer sidewall area
You must know that tires are constructed with steel cords inside their casings, which are covered in rubber for protection, and that a vehicle has this major defect when cords are exposed in the tread or sidewall of any tire.

Procedure:
- Select one tire of the vehicle and inspect it for:
1. Damaged tread or sidewall of tire –(any visual signs such as cuts or other damage to treads and sidewalls)
2. Tire tread depth–to ensure the depth is greater than the minimum allowable depth for the tire positions in vehicle safety regulations (3mm steer tire and 1.5 mm for other tires)
3. Contact with another tire or any vehicle component other than mud flap–to ensure there is no contact
4. Exposed cords in the tread or outer sidewall area–to ensure

there are no exposed cords in the tread or sidewall of any tire

21. Wheels, hubs and fasteners
Hub oil below minimum level (when fitted with sight glass)
You must know that wheel hubs use bearings that require lubrication, that oil is often used as a bearing lubricant, that hub caps used with oil-lubricated bearings may have a clear window allowing a visual inspection of the oil fill level, and that a vehicle has this minor defect when you can see that the hub-oil level is below minimum.

Leaking wheel seal
You must know that wheel hubs require seals to keep the lubricant inside the hub; when a wheel seal is leaking, the wheel bearing can fail, and that a vehicle has this minor defect when there is evidence of a leaking wheel seal.

Evidence of imminent wheel, hub or bearing failure

You must know the normal appearance of wheel and hub components, the visual indications of more serious unsafe conditions, and that a vehicle has this major defect when there is visual evidence that a wheel, hub or bearing failure could occur.

Procedure:

- Where sight glass is present (or describe procedure if not present), inspect the hub-oil level to ensure oil is above the minimum level.
- Inspect to ensure there is no evidence of a leaking wheel seal—look inside the wheel for oil and stains.
- Inspect to ensure there is no visual evidence that a wheel, hub or bearing failure could occur.

22. Wheels, hubs and fasteners

Wheel has loose, missing or ineffective fastener

You must know: the visual features of different types of wheel systems; the importance of keeping wheel fasteners (normally nuts and bolts) properly tightened; be able to detect missing fasteners and recognize the visual signs of loose or ineffective fasteners; and know that a vehicle has this major defect when any wheel has a loose, missing or ineffective fastener.

Evidence of imminent wheel, hub or bearing failure

You must know the normal appearance of wheel and hub components and the visual indications of more serious unsafe conditions, and that a vehicle has this major defect when there is visual evidence that a wheel, hub or bearing failure could occur.

Procedure:

- Inspect for any missing fasteners and recognize the visual signs of loose or ineffective fasteners such as a gap between nut and wheel.

- Inspect to ensure there is no visual evidence that a wheel, hub or bearing failure could occur.

23. Wheels, hubs and fasteners

Damaged, cracked or broken wheel, rim, attaching part

You must know the visual features of different types of wheel systems, the normal appearance of the individual components, and that a vehicle has this major defect when any wheel, rim, or any part used to attach the wheel or rim, is damaged, cracked or broken.

Evidence of imminent wheel, hub or bearing failure

You must know the normal appearance of wheel and hub components, and the visual indications of more serious unsafe conditions, and that a vehicle has this major defect when there is visual evidence that a wheel, hub or bearing failure could occur.

Procedure:

Open hood if access will improve visibility and inspect inner-and-outer wheel assembly to ensure:

- Any wheel, rim, or any part used to attach the wheel or rim, is not damaged, cracked or broken.
- There is no visual evidence that a wheel, hub or bearing failure could occur.

In-cab check

Once the exterior inspection is complete, you will enter the vehicle and begin the in-cab check portion of the test, where you must point to or touch all items and fully explain what you are inspecting for each item. You are not required to list the minor or major defects.

Diagram 6-1

During the in-cab check portion of the test, you will be expected to start the vehicle and perform the following checks:

All the gauges	Confirm and indicate that all gauges and indicators are normal and working properly.
Air pressure gauge (air brake vehicle only)	Confirm and indicate air pressure gauge is working properly and is within normal operating range.
Driver's seat and seat belt	Confirm the driver seat is secure and seat belts are secure, and in good working condition.
Mirror and windshield	Check the windshield and confirm it is clear and has no obstructions or damage to the glass. Confirm the mirrors are properly adjusted.
Heater/defroster controls	Confirm the heater(s) and defroster(s) work in all positions.
Steering wheel	Confirm the steering wheel is securely attached to the vehicle, responds in the normal way and there is no excessive free play.
Wipers and washers	Confirm the windshield wipers and washer fluid are working normally.

Interior inspection

Once the in-cab check is complete, you will find and inspect two randomly generated items from Schedule 1 and be required to:

- Demonstrate and describe how you would inspect the particular item.
- Explain what the defect(s) would be for the particular item.
- Describe what action you would take upon identifying a minor and/ or major defect.

1. Driver seat

Seat is damaged or fails to remain in set position

You must know that the driver seat has to be properly positioned to be able to control the vehicle, know the methods for confirming the seating positions, as well as the locking methods, and that the vehicle has this minor defect when the seat is damaged or won't stay in the position needed to drive.

Seat belt or tether belt is insecure, missing or malfunctions

You must know the importance of seat belts, how to properly wear them and the condition they must be in to function properly. You must know that a vehicle has this major defect when any seat belt or tether belt is insecure, missing or malfunctions.

Procedure:

Inspect:
- Driver seat to ensure it is not damaged and will stay in the position needed to drive.
- Seat belt to ensure tether belt is secure and works correctly clipped and unclipped.

2. Emergency equipment and safety devices

Emergency equipment is missing, damaged or defective

You must know what emergency equipment is required for the type of transport you are involved in, how

to check it, and that a vehicle has this minor defect when any necessary emergency equipment is missing, damaged or doesn't work properly.

Procedure:

- Verbally identify where the emergency flares, lamp or reflectors are located and that they are working properly and secure.

3. Heater / Defroster

Control or system failure

You must know the importance of the heater/defroster always being available for keeping the windshield clear of condensation, and that a vehicle has this minor defect when the heater/defroster system operates incorrectly.

Procedure:

- Turn on heater/defroster fan for all directional controls/positions and ensure the system operates correctly in all positions.

- When applicable, ensure the defroster keeps the windshield clear.

4. Glass and mirrors

Required mirror or window glass fails to provide the required view to the driver as a result of being cracked, broken, damaged, missing or maladjusted

You must know the importance of always having a clear view of the conditions around the vehicle, the windows and mirrors that are required on the vehicle, and that a vehicle has this minor defect when there's mirror- or window-glass damage that reduces this needed visibility.

Procedure:

- Inspect mirrors and windows for any cracks or damage that reduce the required view to the driver, and ensure mirrors are properly adjusted.

5. Windshield wiper/washer

Control or system malfunction

You must know how to operate the windshield wipers and washers, that periodic testing is required to ensure they are available at all times, and that a vehicle has this minor defect when the control or any part of the system fails to function properly.

Wiper blade damaged, missing or fails to adequately clear driver's field of vision

You must know the normal condition and function of wiper blades, and be able to recognize when they no longer function well, and that a vehicle has this minor defect when a wiper blade is damaged or missing, or when it won't clear the area of the windshield in front of the driver.

When use of wipers or washer is required – wiper or washer fails to adequately clear driver's field of vision in area swept by driver's-side wiper

You must know that being able to see the roadway clearly in poor weather is very important, that this visibility is dependent upon the wipers being able to clear water, snow and ice from the windshield, and that a vehicle has this major defect when the prevailing weather conditions require use of the wipers or washers, and they are not able to keep clear the area swept by the driver's side wiper.

Procedure:

Inspect vehicle to ensure:

- The windshield wipers and washers function properly in all directions.
- Any wiper blade is not damaged or missing, and will clear the windshield.

UNCOUPLING AND COUPLING TEST
Overview and procedures

During the uncoupling and coupling portion of the test, you must demonstrate you can safely uncouple and couple a truck/tractor and trailer.

After the daily inspection test, you will exit the vehicle and begin the uncoupling and coupling portion of the test.

The vehicle will be in a pre-determined location that is suitable and safe for uncoupling and coupling the vehicle. You will be asked to perform uncoupling first, followed by coupling.

Refer to page 21-23 for the un-coupling and coupling procedures.

BACKING SKILLS TEST
Introduction
The purpose of the backing skills test is to test skills essential for the safe control of the vehicle while reversing into a desired location, and simulta-neously judging the vehicle's position as it relates to surrounding objects during the exercise.

Examiners will be outside of the vehicle, always visible to you but will not coach or guide you as you are backing.

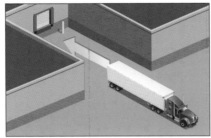
Diagram 6-2

Required backing manoeuvres
You will be required to perform one backing manoeuvre during the test, either a 90-degree alley dock (driver's side), an offset left, or offset right.

Cones will be used to mark the boundaries for each manoeuvre; you must not hit any of them; and your vehicle should be as straight as pos-sible within the cones when complete. You must secure the vehicle and in-form the examiner you are finished.

For proper backing procedure refer to page 39 on backing. During the road test, you will be scored on the following:

- **Observation** – Before backing, you must exit the vehicle to check its path and observe the environment around the vehicle; and while backing, you must use mirrors to check the vehicle path.
- **Signals/Horn** – You must activate the four-way flashers and sound the electric horn before backing.
- **Speed** – Always reverse at a walk-ing pace.
- **Pull-ups** – When you stop and pull forward to get a better position, it is scored as a "pull-up." Stopping without changing direction does not count as a pull-up. You will not be penalized for initial pull-ups. However, an excessive number of pull-ups will count as errors.
- **Final position** – You must back the vehicle as close as possible to the final position.

ON-ROAD DRIVING TEST

You will drive over a test route that has a variety of traffic situations. At all times during the test, you must drive in a safe and responsible manner; and wear your safety belt. Obey all traffic signs, signals and laws. Complete the test without an accident or moving violation. During the driving test, the examiner will be scoring you on specific driving manoeuvres, as well as on your general driving behavior. You will follow the directions of the examiner. Directions will be given to you so that you will have plenty of time to do what the examiner has asked. You will not be asked to drive in an unsafe manner. If your test route does not have certain traffic situations, you may be asked to simulate a traffic situation. You will do this by telling the examiner what you would do if you were in that traffic situation.

As part of the road test you will be expected to drive in a variety of traffic situations including:

- Left and right turns
- Intersections
- Lane changes
- Driving along
- Curves
- Expressway section
- Roadside stop/start

I. LEFT AND RIGHT TURNS

The approach

Traffic check

When approaching a turn, you must monitor the surrounding traffic ahead. Conduct a visual search of the intersection for other vehicles, pedestrians and objects.

Lane change

You must correctly select the lane(s) for entering the intersection. This may involve completing a lane change to get into the appropriate lane.

Signal

You must activate turn signals on approach as soon as appropriate.

Speed

You must gradually slow your vehicle to allow for proper control and to ensure smooth traffic flow.

Transmission/gears

You must select a gear that is appropriate for the vehicle speed and load, and that allows the engine to operate within its normal r.p.m. range.

Lane position

You must plan the correct pathway for entering and exiting the intersection.

If stopping

Smooth stop

You must be aware of traffic conditions and complete a smooth stop.

Full Stop

Keep the vehicle under control while stopped. Do not roll backward or forward.

Stop position/gap

Stop in the proper legal stop position to see the area ahead. Stopping with reasonable space between your vehicle and the vehicle ahead allows you to manoeuvre the vehicle if necessary. Move forward when adequate space becomes available ahead.

Wheels

Keep the wheels straight while waiting to turn. With curved sidewalks, the vehicle can be angled to follow the curb.

Traffic check

Monitor the surrounding traffic ahead. Before entering the intersection, you must check to the left, ahead, to the right and behind to ensure the way is clear.

Turning

Traffic check

Monitor the surrounding traffic ahead, beside and in the mirrors.

Both hands/gears

You must maintain a two-handed grip on the steering wheel as much as possible during an intersection crossing. Minimize gear changes during an intersection crossing, and avoid all unnecessary gear changes. Any grade change in an intersection may also necessitate a gear change to maintain a consistent speed.

Speed/right-of-way

You must complete the turn at a speed appropriate for the conditions. You must recognize and correctly respond to right-of-way obligations in making the turn. Failure to take own right-of-way will impede traffic.

Wide/short

You must follow the path that is appropriate for your vehicle size and length. Do not travel too far away from the normal lane position, to avoid creating unnecessary space.

Complete turn

Traffic check

You must make regular traffic checks to be aware of the traffic patterns that flow around the vehicle (for example, ahead, sides and rear).

Correct lane

You must turn into the lane that corresponds to the lane you were in at the start of the turn. Turn into a lane that permits travel and acceleration without the added burden of attempting a lane change because of parked cars or other obstructions.

Signals/speed/gears

Signals must be cancelled so that other drivers do not get confused. Smooth even acceleration prevents damage to the vehicle. It is important that the vehicle picks up speed and does not delay other traffic.

Moves right

Upon completion of a left turn, you must select the lane that provides the safest unimpeded travel for through traffic.

II. INTERSECTIONS

Stop intersections

The approach

Traffic check

While approaching the intersection, you must monitor the surrounding traffic ahead. Watch for signage, observe traffic-control devices and monitor traffic flow. Respond to potential obstructions or delays that can prevent travelling through the intersection at a normal rate.

Speed

Gradual slowing allows for proper control of the vehicle. To ensure smooth traffic flow and equipment/shipment integrity, you must be aware of traffic conditions and execute smooth manoeuvres.

Transmission/gears

You must select a gear that is appropriate for the vehicle speed and load that allows the engine to operate within its normal r.p.m. range.

Lane position

You must stay in the same lane approaching the intersection and not change position or lanes unnecessarily to ensure traffic flow is smooth and safe.

Stopping

Smooth stop

You must be aware of traffic conditions and execute smooth manoeuvres.

Full-stop roll

Making a full stop allows you enough time to thoroughly observe the traffic environment around the vehicle. You must keep the vehicle under control while stopped. Do not roll backward or forward.

Stop position/gap

Stopping in the proper legal stop position allows you to see the area ahead. Stopping in the intersection may impede the flow of cross traffic. Stopping with enough space between your vehicle and the vehicle ahead allows you to be able to manoeuvre the vehicle if necessary. You must move forward when adequate space becomes available ahead.

Traffic check

While waiting, you must monitor the surrounding traffic ahead, beside and in the vehicle mirrors to alert yourself to any changes in traffic conditions.

Starting

Traffic check

Before entering the intersection, you must monitor the surrounding traffic ahead.

Speed/right-of-way

You must start vehicle movement within a reasonable time when permitted by the traffic light and/or the movement of the vehicle ahead. You must also enter and travel through the intersection in a reasonable time.

Both hands/gears

You must maintain a two-handed grip on the steering wheel. Situations where only one hand is on the wheel must be limited to times when it is necessary to operate other vehicle controls or make a gear selection.

Lane position

You must follow the correct pathway upon entering and exiting the intersection. Do not change lanes or position in the intersection.

Traffic check

Keeping a constant visual search through the vehicle mirrors will alert you to any changes in condition.

Through intersections

The approach

Traffic check

While approaching the intersection, you must monitor the surrounding traffic ahead.

Speed

Maintain speed approaching the intersection to ensure there is not a disruption in traffic flow. If there is any cross traffic that might enter the intersection ahead, you must slow down or cover the brake.

Gap

Safe following distance must be maintained and adjusted to allow for a safe stop.

Lane/position

You must stay in the same lane/ position as you approach the intersection to ensure traffic flow is smooth and safe.

Driving through

Lane/position

You must stay in the same lane/ position as you travel through the intersections to ensure traffic flow is smooth and safe.

Both hands/gears

To maintain proper control of the vehicle, your hands should be on the steering wheel. Any necessary transmission shifts should be made prior to entering an intersection. Downshifting prior to an intersection

may be necessary to avoid lugging the engine.

Traffic check

Checking mirrors after clearing an intersection allows you to be continually aware of conditions so that necessary adjustments in speed and position can be made.

III. LANE CHANGES

Traffic check

In anticipation of making a lane change, you must observe traffic to identify where and when the lane change should be made.

Signal

You must signal to alert other motorists of the intention to change lanes. The signal can be initiated at any reasonable time before the lane change, and must be cancelled when the lane change is complete.

Spacing

You must maintain a safe following distance within your current lane while preparing to make the lane change. The space you will require in the target lane must be adequate for the vehicle's length. You must check mirrors for vehicles travelling alongside, passing or approaching from the rear, and any vehicle that may already be in–or may enter–a blind spot.

Speed

You should operate within 10 km/h of the posted speed limit if conditions permit without exceeding the posted limit.

Changing lane

You must observe road and pavement markings. You must make the lane change at a point of the roadway where road conditions and marking indicate the lane change can be made. Intersections, pedestrian crossings, railway crossings and solid pavement markings are locations that are not suitable for making a lane change.

Lane change motion

The lane change itself needs to be deliberate, but smooth and steady. Sudden lateral movements should be avoided, and taking too much time allows the traffic patterns to change during the lane change. Hesitating may also cause other motorists to change speed or position. The vehicle should be steered into the centre of the target lane, adjusting speed as necessary to establish safe distances from other vehicles.

IV. DRIVING ALONG
Traffic check

You should look well ahead; mirror checks are critical because of the vehicle's large blind spots. You must be continually aware of conditions so that necessary adjustments in speed and position can be made.

Speed

You should operate within 10 km/h of the posted speed limit if conditions permit without exceeding the posted limit.

Spacing

Because of the increased stopping distance of commercial vehicles, you must adjust the following distance to observe, react or manoeuvre the vehicle if necessary. You must also avoid driving beside or in the blind spot of other vehicles. You may need space to suddenly change lanes. When traffic is heavy, avoiding driving beside other vehicles may be difficult.

Lane usage

You should choose the right-most lane that can be travelled safely. Staying as far to the right as possible will minimize the disruption of traffic flow and keep hazards to the left side of the vehicle, where the view is less restricted.

Exiting

Traffic check

You must look ahead for exit signs and be aware of the proper lane to use for exiting, as well as checking ahead, behind, and to the side for traffic when preparing to exit safely.

Signal

The signal should be activated before slowing and while still on the expressway lane so other drivers can prepare or adjust their driving if required. The signal must also be cancelled.

Exit lane

If a lane change is required to move to the exit lane, the move must be deliberate, but smooth and steady.

Speed

You should not be slowing down on the expressway. The exit lane should be used to slow down.

Spacing

Because of the increased stopping distance of commercial vehicles, the following distance must be adjusted to allow you to observe, react or manoeuvre the vehicle if necessary.

V. CURVE

Speed

You must adjust speed to safely negotiate a curve. Drivers inexperienced with the operation of a particular type of vehicle often misjudge the maximum speed with which they can safely negotiate a curve of a given radius. Excessive speed prior to the curve often requires hard braking.

Lane position

Because of the off-tracking of large vehicles, you must approach the curve from an outside position of the lane to keep the rear wheels from cutting across the top of the curve. Failure to do so can cause the rear wheels to leave the road or present a hazard to vehicles in a neighbouring lane.

Traffic check

A constant visual search around the vehicle is necessary to alert yourself to any changes in traffic. Mirror checks are critical because of the vehicle's large blind spots and off-tracking of rear wheels. You must be continually aware of conditions so that necessary adjustments in speed and position can be made. These adjustments take longer in commercial vehicles because of their large size; you must be able to anticipate them as early as possible.

VI. EXPRESSWAY

Entering

Traffic check

To determine a safe opportunity to merge, you must look ahead, in your mirrors and pay attention to the other vehicles on the expressway while accelerating on the on-ramp. It is important to remember that the onus is on you—and not other vehicles—to merge safely onto the expressway.

Signal

The proper signal must be activated early, as soon as other vehicles can see you on the on-ramp, and not cancelled until your vehicle is in the new lane, to give other vehicles time to make any necessary adjustments.

However, keep in mind that you do not have the right-of-way.

Spacing

Because of the increased stopping distance of loaded or empty trucks and other commercial vehicles, the following distance must be adjusted to allow you the ability to observe, react or manoeuvre the vehicle if necessary. You must also stay within the lane markings.

Speed

You should not exceed but travel as closely to the posted ramp advisory speed limit as possible. Use the acceleration lane to gain as much speed as necessary, and reach as closely to the expressway speed as possible.

Merge

The merge needs to be deliberate, but smooth and steady. Sudden lateral movements should be avoided. Taking too much time should also be avoided. The vehicle should be steered into the centre of the target lane while adjusting speed necessary to establish safe distances from other vehicles.

VII. ROADSIDE STOP/START
The approach

Traffic check

While approaching the stop, you must monitor the surrounding traffic ahead.

Speed/gears

Gradual slowing allows for proper control of the vehicle. You must select a gear appropriate for the vehicle speed and load that allows the engine to operate within its normal r.p.m. range.

Signal

Appropriate signals must be used to communicate with other road users, but not too early.

Lane/stop position

Stop as far to the right as possible to minimize disruption of traffic flow, and park so that the vehicle does not restrict vision or cause distractions to other vehicles. Vehicles must be parked parallel and close to the curb or edge of roadway without hitting the curb.

Stopping

Full- stop roll

Once you have reached the final parking position, you must secure the vehicle against movement. It is important that service brakes remain applied until the parking brake is activated.

Signals

The turn signal must be cancelled and the four-way flashers activated so as not to confuse other traffic.

Secure vehicle

For the safety of those around the vehicle, it is important to secure the vehicle against any movement.

Starting

Start

To move the vehicle safely, you must place it in the correct gear and not attempt to pull forward without releasing the brake.

Signals

Cancel the four-way flashers and activate the left-turn signal to warn traffic of the intention to enter the lane. The left-turn signal must be cancelled as soon as you have entered the driving lane.

Traffic check

Observe the traffic environment ahead, left and right, and check mirrors so that you will be alerted to any changes around the vehicle, with checks especially in the direction of the merge.

Speed/gears

Accelerating and merging properly prevents the vehicle from interfering with traffic flow.

Traffic check

Once you have resumed traffic speed, make sure to check the mirrors to be aware of the traffic environment.

You will also be scored on your overall performance in the following categories:

Observation

You must be continually aware of conditions so that necessary adjustments in speed and position can be made. It is important to constantly monitor mirrors to see vehicles approaching and to observe where the vehicle is tracking.

Intersection/railway traffic check

While travelling up to the intersection or railway crossing, you must monitor the surrounding traffic ahead, and beside and to the rear through the vehicle mirrors.

Lane usage

If you observe the environment ahead, you should choose the right-most lane that can be travelled safely. Stay as far to the right as possible. You may also use the next lane if the right-most lane requires constantly changing lanes.

Speed

You should operate within 10 km/h of the posted speed limit if conditions permit without exceeding the posted limit.

Spacing

Following distance must be adjusted to allow you to observe, react or manoeuvre the vehicle if necessary. You must also avoid passing too closely.

Clutch/gears

Proper use of the clutch eliminates unnecessary stress on the drivetrain, which can lead to equipment damage or breakdowns.

Brakes/accelerator

To ensure smooth traffic flow and equipment/shipment integrity, you must be aware of traffic conditions and execute smooth manoeuvres. Gradual slowing also allows proper control of the vehicle.

Steering

Keeping both hands on the wheel is better to be able to control the vehicle during quick evasive manoeuvres. You must maintain a two-handed grip on the steering wheel as much as possible. Situations where only one hand is on the wheel must be limited to times when it is necessary to operate other vehicle controls or make a gear selection.

Turn signals

Signals alert other traffic that you are about to merge, exit or change lanes. Turn signals on most commercial vehicles are not self-cancelling and need to be manually cancelled so other road users are not confused.

CHAPTER 7
ADDITIONAL INFORMATION

I. ONTARIO'S DRIVE CLEAN PROGRAM

Vehicles are a major domestic source of smog-causing emissions in Ontario. Drive Clean, administered by the Ministry of the Environment, reduces smog-causing pollutants by identifying grossly polluting vehicles and requiring them to be repaired. Accordingly, Drive Clean sets up a schedule for when vehicles must be tested.

Drive Clean requires diesel-powered, heavy-duty vehicles registered anywhere in Ontario to be tested annually. Non-diesel, heavy-duty vehicles must be tested annually only if they are registered in the Drive Clean program area (for example, southern Ontario from Windsor to Ottawa).

The Ministry of Transportation will notify you if your vehicle needs a test. Or you can check the Drive Clean website www.driveclean.com or call the Drive Clean Contact Centre at 1-888-758-2999 for more information on the program and test requirements.

Effective September 1, 2011, changes were made that exempt some vehicles from Drive Clean. Please visit the Drive Clean website to see if your vehicle is affected.

Drive Clean offers the owners of diesel vehicles an incentive to be tested every two years, instead of every year. To qualify, your vehicle must register a 20 per cent or lower opacity reading. Vehicles that register over 20 per cent opacity still require annual tests.

If you are buying or selling a used vehicle that is older than the current model year, the vehicle must pass a Drive Clean test so that the ownership can be transferred and the vehicle

can be plated for the road. This requirement helps to ensure that you do not purchase a vehicle with emissions problems.

You don't have to wait for a Drive Clean test to do something positive for the environment. Keeping your vehicle well maintained according to the manufacturer's recommended service schedules is an important part of driving clean. For example, if the "check engine" or "service engine" lights come on, go to a qualified repair technician to have your engine checked as soon as possible. Otherwise, you could face costly repairs to the vehicle's engine or emissions-control system.

All vehicles on Ontario's highways — whether registered in Ontario or out-of-province — are subject to the provincial *environmental protection act*. The Act prohibits excessive visible exhaust emissions and the alteration or removal of

emissions-control equipment. This applies to vehicles even if they have passed a Drive Clean test.

For more information on Ontario's Drive Clean program, visit www.driveclean.com or call the Drive Clean Contact Centre toll-free at 1-888-758-2999.

II. HIGH OCCUPANCY VEHICLE (HOV) LANES

A High-Occupancy Vehicle (HOV) lane is a specially designed lane that is designated for use by certain types of vehicles with a specified number of occupants. It can offer travel-time savings to those who choose to carpool or take transit. HOV lanes can move a greater number of people than a general traffic lane, and encourage carpooling and transit use by providing travel-time savings and a more reliable trip time. HOV lanes are open 24 hours a day, seven days a week.

HOV lanes benefit all drivers, not only those who carpool, in the following ways:
- Improves highway infrastructure by moving more people in fewer cars
- Reduces the number of vehicles on the road
- Reduces vehicle emissions and improves air quality
- Helps you conserve fuel, save money (by sharing the cost of driving) and reduce stress

HOV lanes on provincial highways are reserved for vehicles carrying at least two people (for example, a driver plus one or more passengers in any of the following vehicles: cars, minivans, motorcycles, pickup trucks, taxis, buses and limousines). Note that large trucks are not permitted on the HOV lanes, regardless of the number of occupants.
- The HOV lane is separated from the other general traffic lanes by a striped buffer zone. It is illegal and

unsafe to cross the striped buffer pavement markings.

- Certain vehicles are exempt from the HOV lane rules. Buses can use an HOV lane at any time, regardless of the number of occupants. Emergency vehicles such as police, fire and ambulance are also exempt from the restrictions.
- If you use the HOV lanes improperly, you can be stopped and ticketed by a police officer. You will be required to re-enter the general lanes at the next entry/exit zone.
- Commercial motor vehicles must have two or more people in the vehicle and be less than 6.5 metres in total length to be in the HOV lane. Single-occupant taxis and airport limousines are permitted in the HOV lane until June 30, 2018. Vehicles with the "Green" licence plate are permitted in the HOV lane with any number of occupants. Green plates are available

for eligible plug-in hybrid electric vehicles and full-battery electric vehicles. Please consult the Ministry of Transportation website for more details.

III. DRIVING EFFICIENTLY
Smart driving practices

Fuel efficiency starts when you turn your engine on. Proper warm-up helps lubricate components and seals, reducing wear and leakage. Starting your truck properly can save money on fuel. As a driver, you can help to protect the environment from the harmful effects of driving by following these suggestions:

- When starting your vehicle, make sure you use zero throttle and are in a gear that doesn't need any throttle.
- Don't pump the throttle unnecessarily; the amount of fuel required for starting is pre-measured. Pumping the throttle wastes fuel and can damage cylinder walls.

- Use ether sparingly when having difficulty starting your engine; excessive use can harm the engine.
- Let your vehicle warm up for three to five minutes–if the temperature is below 0 degrees Celsius, allow it warm up for seven to 10 minutes. Do not rev the engine; let it warm up gradually.
- Warm up your vehicle after the initial idle time by driving easily; don't try to get too much speed out of the engine by pushing the throttle down hard.
- Ensure oil and air pressure are in their normal operating ranges during start-up.
- Back off the accelerator when going down a hill; let gravity and momentum do the work.
- Use cruise control where appropriate.
- Change gears smoothly–shifting professionally will result in about 30 per cent improvement in operating costs.

- Always use the clutch; failure to do so can wear down the gear teeth in the transmission.
- Practise progressive gear shifting at approximately 1600 r.p.m. Shifting before you reach the maximum governed r.p.m. reduces equipment wear, decreases noise levels and saves fuel.
- Run the engine in the highest gear range to keep it in a low-rev range.
- Use your retarder properly and turn it off when you don't need it. Allow the terrain to work for you.
- Turn off your engine when you stop for any length of time. You will save fuel, reduce maintenance requirements, prolong engine life and prevent unnecessary emissions.

Fuel-consumption techniques summary:

If you learn and practise the following techniques, you'll be well on the way to good fuel consumption:
- Use good starting procedures.
- Get going as soon as you can.
- Control your idling.
- Be an r.p.m. miser.
- Use progressive shifting.
- Maintain efficient engine speed.
- Manage your road speed.
- Operate efficiently in traffic.

Try our "Check your Green Smarts" quiz to test your knowledge on fuel efficiency. For more information, visit www.fleetsmart.gc.ca.

IV. MANDATORY VEHICLE BRANDING PROGRAM

Under the Mandatory Vehicle Branding Program, insurers, self-insurers (fleet owners), auctioneers, importers, salvagers and anyone who deals in, and takes possession of, used vehicles are required to determine whether severely damaged and written-off ("total loss") vehicles they insure or obtain should be branded either "Irreparable" or "Salvage". They must notify the ministry of the brand through a notification of vehicle brand form. The ministry applies the brand to the vehicle's registration information so that it will appear on the vehicle permit, vehicle abstracts and the used vehicle information package (UVIP) for that vehicle. The brand identifies the condition of the vehicle to potential buyers. This is how the program helps to protect consumers buying used vehicles.

If your vehicle sustains severe damage and is written off by your insurance company, they must notify you and the ministry of the brand requirement. If you do not receive a claim settlement through an insurance company, you must have the brand determined by an authorized mechanic at a Type 6 Motor Vehicle Inspection Station. The ministry website has a list of these facilities–visit mto.gov.on.ca for details.

There are four brands:

- A vehicle that has never had a brand applied in Ontario automatically has the brand "None" applied to its registration documents. However, this does not mean that the vehicle has never been damaged in a collision, was never branded in another jurisdiction or was not rebuilt prior to the mandatory branding program.

- The brand "Irreparable" means that damage to the vehicle was so severe that the vehicle can be used for parts or scrap only. It cannot be rebuilt, and it can never be driven in Ontario.

- The brand "Salvage" means that the damaged vehicle can be repaired or rebuilt. It cannot be registered as fit to drive in Ontario. Once the vehicle has been repaired or rebuilt, and if it can pass a structural inspection to ministry standards, the owner can obtain a structural inspection certificate and have it branded as "Rebuilt".

- The brand "Rebuilt" means that the vehicle has been previously branded as "Salvage", but has been rebuilt and has passed a structural inspection to ministry standards. If the vehicle can pass a safety inspection (Safety Standards Certificate), the owner can have it registered as fit to drive in Ontario.

Motorcycles that have been written off must be branded "Irreparable"; they cannot be branded "Salvage".

Trailers, traction engines, farm tractors, mopeds, motorized snow vehicles, street cars or motor vehicles with a model year of 1980 or earlier are exempt from the mandatory branding program.

V. CHECK YOUR GREEN SMARTS

1. How should you plan your route to increase the fuel efficiency of your vehicle?
a. Select a route "as the crow flies"
b. Choose the shortest way through towns
c. Use bypasses around towns and avoid rush hour
d. Use a single-lane highway

2. Which of these aerodynamic modifications will save more fuel?
a. A trailer mounted device
b. A cab mounted device
c. A side mounted device
d. A cab mounted device with gap-seal deflector

3. When planning a route, which of the following should you take into consideration?
a. The type of road
b. The weather conditions
c. The number of border crossings
d. All of them

4. Driving on snow-covered roads can increase fuel consumption by:
a. 5-10%
b. 10-15%
c. 15%-20%
d. Driving in snow has no effect on fuel consumption

5. What pressure should the tires be inflated to?
a. A standard inflation set by the load that is being carried
b. The inflation recommended by the tire manufacturers
c. 10 psi below the maximum recommended tire pressure
d. 10 psi above the minimum recommended tire pressure

6. Before moving off on a warm day (15°C), how long should you should idle your engine from a cold start?
a. Up to 1 minute
b. 3-5 minutes

c. 2-3 minutes
d. 7-10 minutes

7. Which of the following is the most effective way to save fuel?
a. Avoid idling
b. Reduce speed from 105 km/h to 90 km/h
c. Maintain high engine r.p.m.
d. Use progressive shifting

8. What does the term "Progressive Shifting" refer to?
a. Up-shifting while traveling uphill
b. Downshifting when travelling downhill
c. Shifting at the governed maximum engine r.p.m.
d. Shifting before the engine reaches maximum r.p.m.

9. An idling tractor-trailer engine burns up to:
a. One litre of fuel per hour at 900 r.p.m.
b. Two litres of fuel per hour at 900 r.p.m.
c. Three litres of fuel per hour at 900 r.p.m.
d. Four litres of fuel per hour at 900 r.p.m.

10. With new diesel engines, you should downshift and up-shift at approximately:

a. 1200 and 1600 r.p.m.

b. 1500 and 1800 r.p.m.

c. 1600 and 1900 r.p.m.

d. 1700 and 2000 r.p.m.

Chapter 7-Summary

By the end of this chapter you should know:

- What Ontario's Drive Clean Program is and how it works
- What High Occupancy Vehicle (HOV) lanes are and how they work
- Techniques for driving efficiently and saving fuel
- What the Mandatory Vehicle Branding Program is and how it works

Check your green smarts:

1-c: Plan your route carefully: flat routes are more fuel efficient than mountainous routes; highway driving is more fuel efficient than "inner city" driving.

2-d: Optimize tractor aerodynamics: reducing aerodynamic drag by 10% can increase fuel efficiency by 5%.

3-d: Choosing to drive a flat, multi-lane highway improves your fuel efficiency by:
- 4 to 11% compared to a flat two-lane highway;
- as much as 18% compared to a mountainous highway;
- and 25 to 35% over taking a suburban route.

4-c: Weather conditions affect fuel efficiency. Driving on snow-covered roads can increase fuel consumption by 15 to 20%.

5-b: Ensure your tires are inflated according to the manufacturer's recommendations— 1% of fuel is wasted for each 10 pounds per square inch of under-inflation.

6-b: Let your vehicle warm up for three to five minutes—if the temperature is below 0 degrees Celsius, allow it to warm up for seven to 10 minutes. Do not rev it; let it warm up gradually.

7-b: Reduce your average speed—driving fast eats up fuel no matter what you drive.

8-d: Practise progressive gear-shifting at approximately 1600 r.p.m. Shifting before you reach the maximum governed r.p.m. reduces equipment wear, decreases noise levels and saves fuel.

9-d: Idling a tractor-trailer engine burns up to four litres of fuel per hour at 900 r.p.m.

10-a: New engine designs offer great benefits, delivering more horsepower and torque in lower r.p.m. ranges. You can downshift at about 1200 r.p.m. and up-shift at about 1600 r.p.m.—rather than 2000 r.p.m. You shift less, save money and generate fewer emissions.

INDEX — THE OFFICIAL MTO TRUCK HANDBOOK

CONVERSION CHART

Imperial to Metric Converter

From	To	Multiply By
inches	centimetres	2.54
miles	kilometres	1.61
feet	metres	0.31
pounds	kilograms	0.46
miles per hour	kilometres per hour	1.61

Metric to Imperial Converter

From	To	Multiply By
centimetres	inches	0.39
kilometres	miles	0.62
metres	feet	3.28
kilograms	pounds	2.21
kilometres per hour	miles per hour	0.61

Personalize your licence plates — with two to eight characters, as well as a great choice of colour graphics. Then you'll really stand out from the crowd.

Turn the page to find out more.

NOW THERE ARE MORE WAYS THAN EVER TO EXPRESS YOURSELF!

WE'RE HELPING YOU BUILD CHARACTERS.

Now you've got extra choices when creating your personalized licence plate. We've introduced seven and eight characters. So you've got even more to work with — a minimum of two characters and right up to eight. Just think of the possibilities.

Every personalized plate is one of a kind. No one else can have the same plate as yours.

For more information and to order your personalized plates, call 1-800-AUTO-PL8 (1-800-288-6758).

**Or visit the ServiceOntario website: www.serviceontario.ca
Or drop by your local ServiceOntario centre.**

Gift certificates are available too.

ONTARIO
BCRE8TVE
YOURS TO DISCOVER

ONTARIO
NOWYOURS
YOURS TO DISCOVER

Graphic licence plates are a hit! And now there are more than 40 choices available. Support your favourite Ontario sports team, community or arts organization, professional group or university. Or select a timeless icon like the loon or trillium.

For a totally unique look, add a colour graphic to a personalized plate with up to six characters.

So express yourself — with colour graphics and personalized licence plates.

For more information and to order your plates, call 1-800-AUTO-PL8 (1-800-288-6758).

Or visit our website: www.mto.gov.on.ca
Or drop by your local ServiceOntario centre.

Gift certificates
are available too.

ADD SOME COLOUR WHERE IT COUNTS.

OTHER MTO PUBLICATIONS FOR YOU

Copies of this handbook and others may be purchased from a:
- Retail store near you
- DriveTest Centre
- ServiceOntario Centre
- By calling (416) 326-5300 or 1-800-668-9938 (toll free)
- www.serviceontario.ca/publications

Prepayment required by credit card - VISA or Mastercard.
You may also pay with a certified cheque, bank draft or money order at DriveTest Centres.

Handbook and road map prices are subject to applicable H.S.T and shipping handling costs.

THE OFFICIAL DRIVER'S HANDBOOK

THE OFFICIAL MOTORCYCLE HANDBOOK

THE OFFICIAL TRUCK HANDBOOK

THE OFFICIAL BUS HANDBOOK

THE OFFICIAL AIR BRAKE HANDBOOK

THE OFFICIAL ONTARIO ROAD MAP